Michael Grose is one of Australia's most popular writers and speakers on parenting and family matters. The author of four books for parents he has written in excess of 200 columns that have appeared in newspapers and magazines throughout Australia. He also gives over 80 presentations a year throughout Australia promoting healthy family relationships within schools, the workplace and the broader community. With humour and empathy Michael shows parents how to raise happy, confident kids and enjoy family life.

A former primary teacher he has worked with children all his professional life. Young Leaders, his popular leadership program for young people, is conducted in schools in every state in Australia.

Michael is married with three children aged fifteen, fourteen and twelve and lives on the Mornington Peninsula near Melbourne.

For more information and practical ideas to help you raise happy, resilient children and young people visit Michael's website: www.Parentingideas.com.au

GREAT IDEAS FOR (*Tired*) PARENTS

MICHAEL GROSE

RANDOM HOUSE AUSTRALIA

For my parents

Random House Australia Pty Ltd
20 Alfred Street, Milsons Point, NSW 2061
http://www.randomhouse.com.au

Sydney New York Toronto
London Auckland Johannesburg

First published 1994
This Random House Australia edition published 2000

National Library of Australia
Cataloguing-in-Publication Data

Grose, Michael, 1955–
    Great ideas for tired parents.

    ISBN 1 74051 023 2.

    1. Parenting. I. Title.

649.1

Typeset by Midland Typesetters, Maryborough, Victoria
Printed and bound by The SOS Printing Group Pty Ltd

10 9 8 7 6 5 4 3 2

Contents

Acknowledgements

Thank you to Sue, Sam, Emma and Sarah for your support. Special appreciation to Stella, Linda, Josie and Bronwyn for opening a window to a side of parenting that I was unaware of. Appreciation to Mark McKeon for sound ideas on physical fitness and Barbara Lorback for sensible advice about nutrition.

INTRODUCTION

Why am I so tired?

Imagine reading the job advertisement below in a newspaper.

POSITION AVAILABLE

Full-time: long days, seven days a week, some time off in the evenings.

We are seeking a kind, considerate person for the challenging position of parent.

This position requires a competent self-starter with excellent communication skills.

Must be able to provide an atmosphere of love and support.

The ability to be flexible and adaptable is essential.

Strong leadership skills an advantage.

A willingness to put yourself second is required.

Entertainment skills would be a help although not essential.

Must be able to work with limited supervision.

An ability to learn is essential as training is definitely on the job.

Current driver's licence would be an advantage.

Qualifications and experience are not necessary, although you will be fulfilling some or all of the tasks of the following trained people: chef, teacher, medical worker, social worker, psychologist, childcare worker, taxi driver, sales representative, manager, entertainer and nutritionist.

This is an honorary position.

Who would apply for such a job?

The role of parents is multifaceted, as they are both providers and housekeepers, with the responsibility of teaching children appropriate behaviours and skills. Parents must also help children to deal with any difficulties they experience as they grow and mature. As providers of unconditional love, parents often bear the brunt of children's anger, self-doubts and feelings of inadequacy. It is difficult to be a friend to your children and encourage them when they take out their anger on you.

Did I do the right thing when I disciplined my child? Was I fair? Why does she behave in such a way? Parents are frequently full of self-doubt and often question their child-rearing practices. Parents are generally on a sharp learning curve, particularly with the first child in the family. Raising children is a difficult, demanding task that requires patience and stamina, so parenting is definitely for those prepared for the long haul.

Raising children is labour-intensive. Despite the increase in household labour-saving devices, parents are as busy today as they have ever been. Parents not only raise children, tend a household or hold down a job, they also drive kids to sports practice, ballet, music or language lessons. Parents often complain that they have little time to themselves. They are constantly competing with the demands of children, spouses or employers and they have little time to pursue their own interests and look after their minds and bodies as they would like.

The nature and shape of families have changed dramatically over the last few decades. Approximately twenty per cent of families are now headed by a sole parent. The increase in divorce and separation rates has seen a rise in the number of stepfamilies. Families where both parents work are now common rather than the exception, as they were a generation ago, and more men are assuming the major responsibility for raising children than ever before. These changes merely add new dimensions to the demands already placed on parents as we begin this new millennium.

This book acknowledges the fact that parents are extremely busy people. The quality of parenting has as much to do with general well-being as it has with knowledge, skill and child-raising techniques. Parents owe it to themselves and their children to remain physically fit, mentally fresh and spiritually healthy.

It's up to you

You *can* take control of the way you live. This is a constant theme throughout this book. You may not be able to control other people such as partners, children and friends, or the many unexpected situations that occur on a regular basis. However, you can take charge of your own actions and attitudes. One of the most challenging aspects of parenting is being able to maintain yourself physically, mentally and spiritually. There are many competing demands but the responsibility for looking after yourself belongs to you. Permit yourself to come first some of the time and be confident that a healthy, interesting, more vital person will do a far better job than a jaded parent who is falling apart at the seams.

Great Ideas for Tired Parents is all about making the job of raising children easier and helping parents cope with the demands of a joyous yet difficult task. Good luck and happy parenting!

Michael Grose

Chapter 1

EXPLODING THOSE MYTHS

Have you ever asked yourself why you did something and all you could answer was 'Because I had to'? Many myths and misconceptions exist that complicate our lives as parents. Some are learned from our own parents while others are gained from friends, books and the media. Some myths we work out on our own, while many remain unchallenged.

Misconceptions and unfounded beliefs often dictate the way we raise children. They cause the 'I have to . . .' syndrome which places enormous pressure on our lives. I want to challenge and explode some of the myths (thirteen common ones are outlined in this chapter) which exist to make our lot as parents difficult.

My children must come first in my life

It's true that the arrival of children leads to a change of priorities and significant lifestyle changes. Nights out with your partner become less frequent and spur-of-the-moment visits are a thing of the past. For me, going to the movies took a back seat for a while, although I became an avid video watcher. Social lives need more planning than in the pre-children days. Raising children does require some sacrifices but these should not include our own and our partner's needs.

We have a responsibility to look after ourselves physically, mentally and spiritually. Kids don't need a mother or father who is worn out or frustrated because they are living their lives for or through their children. Kids want parents who are happy and able to give freely of themselves because they want to. We are not just parents, housekeepers and breadwinners. We have a responsibility to ourselves and, if we have one, to that other person in our lives — our partner. We need intimacy that cannot be fulfilled by our children. Kids benefit from parents who lead satisfying lives which revolve around things other than children.

Children need to learn that their interests and needs compete with your own. 'Can I go to Ella's place to play, mum?' 'No dear, I'm going to jazz ballet classes after school. I can't be in two places at once.' Develop the habit of saying no to children to maintain some time for yourself and your own interests.

I have no time for myself

This is the tired parents' motto. Avoid the guilts because you are not tending your baby. This is useless thinking. You will have no time for yourself and your interests unless you make the time. Sure, it takes planning and effort to give yourself some 'own time' but it's worth it. Create some regular time for yourself in your routine. Use occasional babysitters, creche, friends, a relative or your partner (see Support network, pages 45–50) to give you a break so that you can pursue personal interests. The children will survive without you.

I am responsible for my children's behaviour

What a heavy burden to carry! This means that if you had five children, say, that would be six people to be held responsible for. Life would be unbearable!

To hold ourselves responsible for all our kids' misdemeanours is to forget one important fact — they have minds of their own and choose to behave in various ways. Children will misbehave to gain attention, as a display of personal power, to define the boundaries of acceptable activity, and sometimes due to boredom.

Kids do not act in a vacuum. They will alter and assume responsibility for their behaviour when they experience the consequences of their actions. A toddler will refrain from entering her parents' bedroom at night if she is consistently returned to her own bed.

It's important to shift the responsibility for behaviour

to where it belongs. Parents often shield kids from the results of their behaviour in the belief that they're doing what is best. The parent who keeps a son's meal warm when he is constantly late home is taking responsibility for the son's tardiness.

I must control my child

This is the impossible dream of many parents. Like Don Quixote, parents who believe that they can control their child's behaviour will forever be tilting at windmills. Most children resist parents' efforts to control their behaviour at some stage. Many meekly comply with their parents' wishes for the first twelve or so years and explode like a bomb when they reach adolescence. 'You want me to get a haircut, I'll grow it long. You like my new hairstyle, I'll cut it short.'

It's not only teenagers who go to great lengths to demonstrate their independence. Watch a youngster procrastinate when you want him to do a job for you. A small protest that lets you know he will do it for you in his time. Infuriating yes, surprising no!

Recognise that you cannot make a child do anything that he doesn't want to do. I know this is extremely difficult for most of us to believe, but by controlling our behaviour we are able to stimulate, influence and guide our children into choosing acceptable behaviours.

I must be seen to be a good parent

There are two separate issues to be discussed with this myth. The first deals with the idea of 'being seen', or the perceptions that are maintained. The second issue relates to the notion of the 'good' parent.

Being seen. Some parents place great importance on other people's perceptions of them. During a talk I gave to a group of parents a couple of years ago on promoting responsibility in children, I mentioned that at times it may be appropriate to take dawdling children to preschool, even if they weren't fully dressed. They could finish dressing in the car once at school or even in the preschool if they chose.

A mother in the audience immediately replied, 'I couldn't do that! What would the others think of me?' I realised that it is pointless arguing or trying to convince anyone of the merits of such a ploy when their main concern is with the parental image being projected. It's impossible to control how others think about us, so why bother? The only person who you can really please is yourself.

Being a 'good' parent. 'Good' parents protect children from many of life's difficulties. They take lunch to school when it is forgotten, believe that chores are something for parents rather than children, and shield kids from the consequences of their misbehaviour. 'Good' parents have the best of intentions, but in their desire to do what is best for their kids they often rob them of opportunities to develop independence and responsibility. The alternative is to be a 'responsible' parent.

Responsible parents don't shield kids from consequences; a forgotten lunch is not taken to school, as they have faith in their child's ability to cope with such a small inconvenience. They help children resolve problems by offering suggestions rather than resolving any difficulties. More importantly, they believe children are capable of dealing with many of life's difficulties without falling apart.

Responsible parents also don't look at other people's children as measuring sticks for their own performance as parents. High ideals to live up to, but worth aiming for.

Good children do not misbehave

All children misbehave, some are just more noticeable than others. Often during parent–teacher interviews I commented to parents about the cooperative behaviour of their child, only to receive looks of disbelief. 'She's well behaved? Are you sure you have the right child? Jessica can be really difficult at home. What a surprise!' Children can often be angels in one setting and devils in another.

Kids of all ages constantly test the boundaries they operate within at home and at school. They generally know through experience or observation how far they can stretch the limits in most situations. They know that mum may be able to put up with a great deal of noise inside the house, whereas dad can't stand any racket whatsoever. By testing and crossing the boundary of acceptable behaviour, children learn to predict and regulate their ways of acting.

There is no such creature as the perfect child, just as there is no such person as the perfect parent. How boring life would be if children were perfect!

Children need our assistance most of the time

Children are extremely capable; just watch a child who really wants something. He will overcome all obstacles to get it. I remember my daughter as a four-year-old go to enormous lengths to get an ice-cream after I refused her one.

I was intrigued as I watched her push a chair up next to the refrigerator, climb up, remove the ice-cream tub from the freezer, scoop out enough to feed the whole family, return the ice-cream to the freezer, return the chair to its place and clean up the mess with a sponge. She then ate her ice-cream in her room in an effort to avoid detection, put her bowl in the dishwasher, washed her face and hands then sat next to me in the living room.

Five minutes later she asked me for a drink of water. When I suggested that she might get it herself she replied, 'I can't reach the tap, dad.' I was stunned. Who was fooling whom? I won't fall for that one again!

Many parents underestimate their kids' ability to handle problems such as leaving lunches at home, or facing a school bully, to name a few. Our role as parents is to support children, offer advice and ideas to enable them to cope, but not to take over their problems or to solve them. It is more effective to provide kids with the skills necessary to handle life's problems.

Life should always be fair

'Dad, Stephanie had an ice-cream and I didn't. That's not fair.'

'Yes, Jesse, I bought your sister an ice-cream. She was with me at the shop so I bought her a little treat.'

'But I didn't get one.'

'But Jesse, you were out with your mother. You weren't with me.'

'Yeah, but Stephanie had an ice-cream and I didn't get a treat. That's not fair.'

'Alright, I'll go to the shop and buy you a treat.'

The lengths we often go to for the sake of fairness!

Kids often meet with unfair circumstances — unjust punishments at school, being overlooked for a sports team, or having items stolen. It's a natural reaction to protect our children from such injustices or to over-compensate for disappointments.

However, it's better to help them cope than to over-compensate for the sake of fairness. Those children who move on rather than become obsessed with fairness are usually more successful and lead happier lives. When they come home from school wailing, 'The teacher kept us all in because some of the boys were being silly. That's not fair!, we can agree with them wholeheartedly and add, 'You're right. That's not fair. But many other things aren't fair either.'

Competition brings out the best in children

The myth of the competitive ethic needs to be exposed as it brings out kids' worst qualities. Competition is fine on the sports field but it should be banned from families and the classroom for good. When we compete there are winners and losers. If we measure our worth by the number of people we can be smarter, faster or funnier than, then we are bound to be disappointed, as there will always be people better and brighter than us. It is better to be the best runner, student or actor you can be, regardless of how you measure up to others.

Competition and cooperation don't mix. The greatest challenge for kids is to learn how to cooperate with each other, their parents and teachers. They need to function for the good of the group rather than for their own benefit.

Look at two competitive siblings in a family. One is a capable reader while the other one struggles. Will the good reader spend time with the struggling reader to improve his skills? Not likely. A competitive child will work to maintain this distance rather than try to narrow the gap. His worth is measured by being better than others, not by being the same.

Kids won't try if they're not certain they'll succeed. Competitive children usually are low risk-takers. They only pursue activities where they can dominate or at best do well, and refuse to participate in activities where they won't shine.

Children don't need competition to bring out the best in them. Success is a strong motivator for children. When they experience success kids will generally extend themselves to their fullest capabilities. Success breeds further success. Look at a child who achieves something significant in school. He is generally pleased with himself and will raise himself to another level, as he has faith in his own capabilities and enjoys the feeling of success. 'I can do it and it feels good.'

Avoid comparing children. 'Peter, why can't you keep your room tidy like your sister?' Many parents make the mistake of comparing children to set an example. This not only discourages kids but breeds competition. Peter might well think, 'I can't be as good as my sister, so I'll be worse.'

I must always have a tidy home

To have children and a tidy home is a contradiction in terms. It is unrealistic to expect to always maintain a neat home. This only adds extra pressure to your lot as a parent and is extremely annoying for children. Kids almost by definition are 'messniks', as their idea of tidiness differs greatly from that of most adults. It can be frustrating to clean a room only to find it cluttered with toys five minutes later. 'Why did I bother?' thinks an exasperated parent.

I'm not suggesting that we abandon standards of cleanliness, but as part of living in a family, kids need to learn to play in ways that minimise mess. Make sure you have at least one tidy space to escape to for a while or to entertain unexpected visitors who drop in for a chat.

A family friend who lives in a small flat always keeps

the kitchen table free from mess for the sake of visitors who may drop in. She has two small children and limited space, so this is the best she can do. You know what? We love to visit and spend time with her as she is warm, caring and humorous. We go to talk to her, not to see her living conditions.

Raising children is a chore

Not long ago I witnessed two fathers who took their kids to swimming lessons at a nearby pool (I was there for the same reason). One father viewed his involvement as a chore while the other obviously enjoyed the lessons and took the opportunity to relax.

The 'chore' father was short-tempered and spoke aggressively to his children, indicating he would rather be elsewhere. The other father took an interest in his kids' swimming, chatted with the other parents and read the newspaper. It would be foolish to read too much in this situation about either parent. However, it was obvious that the attitude of each parent to swimming duty was influencing their well-being.

We can see raising kids as a chore or pleasure. Sure, in reality it's both. If we see parenting as more of a chore, then it is necessary to examine our motives for beginning a family. Did we have our children because we wanted to or because we were expected to? Kids add another dimension to our lives rather than detract from the way we live.

Life will return to normal when the children are older

Does this mean that normal life is suspended while kids are around? Having children *is* life. It is better to make the most of it and enjoy them while they're young. Life will not necessarily be better when children are older or when they've left the nest, it will just be different.

It amazes me how many mothers and fathers I know complain loudly about how their lives have been turned upside-down by the arrival of kids and longingly yearn for the good old days before children. These same parents wear out cameras taking photos of their children. Presumably so they can look back in years to come and reflect on the bad old days when their children were young!

Rather than look to the future when life may be easier, look at the fabulous moments with children — first words, first steps, learning to talk, the happiness and expectations of starting school, losing teeth, reading stories . . . the list goes on and on. Life with children is normal and is to be treasured, not wished away in the hope that times will be easier.

I am not a good parent if I return to work

Participation in the workforce of mothers with children under four has seen a huge increase in recent decades. This is mainly due to economic pressures and the desire of many women to maintain careers rather than relinquish or put them on hold until children are off their hands. Both reasons are legitimate, yet society can be very harsh on women who return to the workforce.

Very few cultures believe that parents, and mothers in particular, should have exclusive rights to rearing children, yet our society seems to be extremely successful at making mothers who return to the workforce feel guilty.

In the last few years the spotlight has been thrown on dads who work excessive hours taking them away from their children. The notion of busy dads are bad dads has gained currency in recent years. While there is no doubt that work can be an impediment to successful fathering men can successfully lead busy working lives and be effective, loving fathers as well.

When mothers return to work before children are at school they are turning their children over to the care of other adults. This exposure can have positive effects for both mother and child. Other adults can offer children a lot in terms of quality care, stimulation and social contact.

It is essential to have confidence in the quality and nature of the care that your child will receive, or your anxiety will spill over into your workplace and caregiving and your life will become intolerable.

Chapter 2

RECHARGING THE BATTERIES

This chapter explores how we can refuel ourselves physically, mentally and spiritually so that we are able to cope with the demands of raising children while balancing other areas of our lives. Parenting is a balancing act between meeting the needs of children, and other adults, and satisfying our own personal needs. No matter whether we are a primary caregiver (someone who takes the major responsibility for raising children), a working parent, a sole parent or in a dual parent situation, it's essential that we attend to our own needs.

Estelle, a mother of three young children, was a tired parent. She didn't exercise enough, she ate poorly, lacked self-confidence and felt extremely stressed trying to be a good mother and wife, as well as keep the books for her husband's small business. Estelle spent so much time in the service of other people that she had forgotten one very important person — herself. She also had no outside interests or hobbies and no viable support network.

Estelle came to a parenting seminar to get some help raising her children. However, an update in parenting techniques would not alleviate her difficulties — she was worn out. Estelle's lifestyle needed an overhaul and her priorities required some rethinking before she could feel in control of her life.

My first suggestion was for Estelle to place herself first, as everyone else in her family came first and she came a distant last. Estelle admitted that she had difficulty with the idea, and realised she would have to learn a word she had forgotten how to use: 'No'. She needed to find time for herself.

Estelle's plight is common among many parents who give so much of themselves that they become worn out. Children tend to be takers who drain us physically, mentally and spiritually. There is nothing wrong with this. They deserve a decent slice of us, but if we give all the time without providing the opportunity to replenish our stocks, we will have nothing left. We become so tired and stale that not only do we feel grumpy and boring to live with, but we have difficulty coping with the demands of daily living. We need to recharge our batteries on a regular basis.

There is no off-season or weekend for parents. It is a full-time task with very little time off. Even when children are at school and a caregiver is not in the workforce, a great deal of time is spent maintaining the house, repairing clothes, preparing meals, attending excursions and generally being of service to children. Not on your life, I hear you say. Good! That means you have placed yourself as top priority and are already recharging your batteries so you can attack the many parenting tasks with enthusiasm and vitality.

Looking after the body corporate

What are our needs? The basic needs such as food, shelter and clothing are obvious, and we attend to these as a matter of course. We also have the desire to love and be loved, to feel worthwhile and to stay healthy. Yes, healthy. We spend a great deal on health care as individuals and collectively as a nation, yet basic health care is cheap and preventative. It begins at home when we look after our basic requirements of exercise, nutrition, relaxation and sleep.

Nutrition

Food is fuel for the body. It helps keep the body healthy for our long-term existence, as well as providing energy to survive each day. Parents normally work a long, arduous day that begins early and ends when the children are in bed. We need plenty of stamina to negotiate these twelve- to fourteen-hour days. A nutritionally balanced diet will provide the necessary energy to get us through the day.

Consider the typical eating pattern of many tired, busy people. They often skip meals, eat on the run or while they're doing something else. They might eat two light meals during the day and overcompensate by eating a huge meal in the evening. This pattern is custom-made for ill-health. Sooner or later their body will crash and a longer time will be spent recuperating from a cold, infection or some other ailment, which forces them to stop and look after their body for a while.

A nutritionally balanced diet requires substantial thought and planning but will soon become a habit. A balanced diet requires that we eat three meals a day, choosing from each of the four main food groups outlined below for each meal.

A balanced diet

These four food groups comprise a balanced meal when combined.

Group 1 Protein foods
Meat, chicken, fish, milk, cheese, lentils, soy products

Group 2 High carbohydrate foods
Bread, cereal, rice, pasta, maize, oats

Group 3 Fruit and vegetables

Group 4 Fats and oils
Butter, olive/vegetable/peanut oil

Breakfast. This is the most important meal of the day, so give it due consideration. If we think of its true meaning, 'breaking the fast', then we get some of idea of its importance. It is possibly twelve hours since we last ate, so the body really does require substantial refuelling to set us up for the day. A nutritious breakfast, consisting of a high-fibre cereal with milk, a piece of fruit, wholemeal or wholegrain toast with a spread and a drink, is cheap and easy to prepare and provides the essential nutrients to prepare for the day ahead.

Lunch. The midday meal should consist of high-protein and carbohydrate foods such as soup, a toasted sandwich or an egg. A substantial lunch helps to maintain the blood-glucose level, which is important if we wish to survive the manic hours before dinnertime. A missed or even a light lunch will generally mean that we feel hungry around four o'clock when we need our energy most.

Dinner. The evening meal should be light, such as a small portion of lasagna (which can be prepared in advance and frozen) accompanied by a salad, with fresh fruit and maybe ice-cream for dessert. It is better to eat less at night rather than in the morning as our evening activities generally use up less energy than those during the day. As a general rule, eat like a king or queen at breakfast, a prince or princess at lunch, and a pauper at night.

Snacks. When you're in need of a quick pick-me-up, try a fortified milk drink. Dried or fresh fruit and nuts are also a healthy and quick alternative. Steer clear of snack foods high in sugar as they provide a quick high but soon leave you feeling tired again as they are quickly digested and pass through the bloodstream at a rapid rate.

A balanced diet is essential for maintaining stamina and helping you to cope with stress during a busy day.

Develop a menu plan

It's five o'clock and your seven-year-old daughter asks, 'What's for tea?'

'Good question, Tanya. I have no idea. Hang on, what have we got in the fridge?'

Five o'clock is no time to be making a decision about dinner. You're probably hungry and will make decisions based on how you feel and what food is available. Besides, the added stress of deciding on a suitable meal at a busy time of the day is something you can do without.

Planning ahead. During a quiet time, plan the meals that the family will eat during the week. You need only do this for evening meals as breakfast and lunch often take care of themselves.

• A meal plan provides an excellent time-saving list for you at the supermarket. Make sure that there is enough variety and nutrition in your meal plan, and that you only have to cook three or four times a week.

• Each time you cook, double the ingredients and freeze or refrigerate the unused half for another night.

• If you want variety, alter the accompaniments, so that if you had vegetables with fish on Monday, prepare rice or a salad when you eat fish on Thursday.

• Remember that fruit and vegetables are interchangeable within a weekly menu plan. Rather than fighting with a child over eating vegetables at a particular meal consider serving fruit for dessert instead.

Don't be overly concerned about serving up the same dish to children in the one week. They require nutritious meals, not gourmet specials. Kids tend to be unadventurous eaters, only eating food that they readily recognise. A specially cooked meal is often met with, 'What is this stuff? I'm not eating this. I want spaghetti.' So be it.

Exercise

We don't have to be fit to be healthy but we do need exercise to stay well. There is a belief in our society that only fitness fanatics exercise. A group dressed in sweat suits and joggers running through the streets are branded as fitness freaks. This is crazy thinking, as you don't have to be a fanatic to benefit from exercise. Exercise is an enjoyable activity which, practised on a regular basis, leads to a feeling of well-being. Experts tell us that regular exercise helps us to live longer. This is great, but it also helps us feel better today. Exercise revitalises us so that we are more able to cope with our daily demands — it is one of the best and cheapest forms of stress release.

Exercise breaks the fatigue cycle. 'But I'm too tired to exercise. I don't have the energy. When I do get time to myself all I want to do is sit down and put my feet up.'

This is a natural reaction to lethargy, but we have to give a bit to get a bit of energy. Exercise may require an initial adjustment to your lifestyle; however, the rewards will far outweigh the small inconvenience you may feel at first.

Starting up — the hardest part

Exercise should be fun. Despite all the good reasons why we should exercise, the reality is that we won't exercise unless we enjoy it, so it's important to choose enjoyable activities. If you're like me and hate jogging, try swimming, walking or organised activities such as aerobics or dancing. Find an exercise partner as it's much easier to find excuses when you exercise alone.

The out and back walk

This activity is a personal favourite as it only takes twenty minutes and adds an element of challenge which I enjoy. It's designed for walkers but can be done just as easily by jogging, running, cycling or, for the more adventurous, rollerblading. If you're finding it difficult to exercise without the kids, why not take them along, whether they're in a pram or walking? You can always throw a frisbee or bounce a ball for them while on your walk.

Pick out a starting point near your home. A tree, your letterbox or a street corner will do. Look at your watch, then walk for ten minutes. When ten minutes have elapsed, make a mental note of the point you've reached, then turn around and retrace your route. The challenge is
continued

---

to make it back to your starting point before the next ten minutes is up. One trick is to take it relatively easily In the first ten minutes.

A week later, return to the same starting point. You now have two challenges. Firstly, you have to walk further in the first ten minutes to pass your previous record (your outmark), and if you do so, you'll have to make it back in the second ten minute segment.

You'll be amazed how much you will improve while you're still able to make it back to the start within your time limit This activity will never take longer than twenty minutes, and will take less time as you improve. If you have been taking it especially easy lately, you may start with five minutes out and back and progress from there.

One final point. As you need to use the same course each time, think about the route you choose. A pleasant location, free from vicious dogs, traffic pollution and intersections, would be an advantage.

How not to quit. When starting out, it is important not to overdo exercise, as this is a recipe for quitting. Exercise three times a week for twenty to thirty minutes. That's only one to one-and-a-half hours a week, which is less than one per cent of your time. Vary your exercise, as the more options you have, the more likely you'll be to make an effective choice. A walk around the park on Monday, a game of keepings-off with the kids on Wednesday and a bike ride on the weekend will satisfy all the requirements of an exercise program.

Finally, don't take exercise too seriously. There have been volumes written about exercise and fitness, and there are formulae such as F-I-T, where F is for Frequency (three times per week), I is for intensity (the heart rate is increased to about 120 beats per minute) and T is for Time (at least twenty continuous minutes). Forget most of that and enjoy yourself. Exercise to the point where you can still breathe evenly enough to carry on a conversation. If you can only . . . talk . . . as intermittently . . . as this text . . . is written, then you're overdoing it. So slow down and have fun.

Relaxation

Daily life can seem like a never-ending race that we never quite win. We are always at the back of the pack trying to catch up. As parents we lead extremely busy lives, despite the great array of labour-saving devices available. And more parents are employed than ever before. Consequently, the number of roles and jobs to be performed by parents has increased rather than decreased. Add to this the increase in the amount of organised activities for children and we find that it's little wonder parents feel they are on a merry-go-round that hardly ever stops.

Parents are often on the go all day. Twelve- to fifteen-hour days are normal for many parents. That feeling of letting go when the children are in bed is something to be savoured. However, you should learn to grab snatches of time during the day, and to take small breaks so you can really relax and get off the treadmill for a time.

Learn to recognise when your body is suffering stress. Do you make fists or grind your teeth? Does your brow furrow and your eyes squint or do your blink incessantly or press your thighs together? Whatever your idiosyncrasy, most of us display some recognisable sign that we are under pressure, overly fatigued or simply in need of a break. Read your body signs and train yourself to relax, even for just a short time. Your batteries should be recharged as often as possible during the day.

Each of us has an innate ability to relax. Unfortunately, our conscious mind can and often does override this protection system. We place much unwanted pressure on ourselves when we think in terms of 'I must' or 'I have to'. We simply need to remind our conscious mind to allow itself to slow down. Relaxation is habit-forming, and it's a skill that requires practice. If you have difficulty relaxing, try this ten-minute breathing exercise below at least three times a day, or whenever you are feeling stressed or overstretched.

Treat yourself. It's almost as good as a massage.
This simple relaxation routine takes about ten minutes at the most but the benefits are worth it. You will feel refreshed and ready to take on the issues of the day.

How to relax, part one

I Find a quiet place (close the bedroom door if you wish).

2 Sit, or even lie down.

3 Close your eyes to remove visual distractions.

4 Breathe in deeply and think to yourself 're', then exhale and think 'lax', 'Re ... lax, re ... lax'.

5 Make your breathing as even and soothing as you can, so that you allow yourself to relax for a minute or two. There is no need to cross your legs, invoke religious incantations or smoke a peace pipe. You are simply giving your conscious mind an instruction, in the same way you implore yourself to think when trying to remember a phone number, a place or a name.

How to relax, part two

I Stop and write down what you were doing so you won't be anxious about forgetting important tasks.

2 Find a quiet place and lie down. Put on some relaxing music if you wish.

3 Let all your muscles go loose one by one, as if you're a rag doll.

4 Starting with your toes, tense for five seconds and relax for ten seconds. Repeat this procedure until your feet feel loose.

5 Now work up your body repeating step 4; calf muscles

continued

next; then your thighs and bottom; your hips and stomach; your chest and back; your fingers, hands and arms; then your shoulders, neck and finally your jaw, face and forehead. When you reach your head you may wish to start again or work your way back down your body.

6 Concentrate on breathing deeply and easily.

7 When you feel totally relaxed, open your eyes, find your list and continue with your daily activities.

Sleep

It may seem obvious that we need to get enough sleep in order to function; however, sleep for many parents is something in short supply. Many parents, particularly mothers of young babies, become so used to lack of sleep that they think it's normal to feel tired all the time. It's not normal, nor is it healthy to trudge from task to task in a zombie-like stupor. If lack sleep is a problem then it's important for your well-being and long-term health to do something to rectify the situation.

It may mean grabbing snatches of sleep in the middle of the day when the baby is asleep, sharing the load with a partner when the kids wake up in the middle of the night for a feed or comfort, or even using a babysitter or a creche for a well-earned rest from time to time (see Support network, page 45). Sleep is a high priority for any parent, particularly one who is feeling overstretched.

Maintaining your well-being

Just as our body gets run-down, we can also get mentally stale, which causes our self-confidence to take a dive. This is common for busy parents who forget to maintain social contacts and neglect to keep up interests or hobbies. Socialising, taking regular breaks from children and receiving encouragement help maintain our self-confidence and general well-being.

We often find it difficult to separate ourselves from the role of parent. At times it's easy to forget the person we were before children came on the scene and turned our lives upside-down. Think back to those pre-children days. Chances are you led a full social life and pursued a number of hobbies and interests.

The responsibility of raising children, often combined with juggling a job, means less time devoted solely to ourselves. This is natural, but it doesn't mean that we should not provide time for ourselves. It merely means we have to plan more than we did before becoming parents.

It's all in the planning. For years I have watched jealously as a relative and his partner who chose to delay having children enjoyed active personal and social lives. I privately thought, their time will come. They can't have it so good all the time.

Well, their time has come and they're learning to cope with less personal time. Sensibly, they have adjusted rather than abandoned their social and personal lives. They love their baby and they also value their time together, so they provide regular time-out for each other (see Partner time-out, page 42) and hire a local babysitter so that they can spend time together seeing a movie or having dinner once a week.

Give yourself a regular break

Allow yourself to take a regular break from your children. It's a necessity rather than a luxury. When we had our first child it was suggested we place him in family daycare for an hour or two each week to give my wife a break. 'No way! I couldn't do that. I would feel guilty and it would be impossible to enjoy myself', she replied. By the time our second child arrived our first-born was a seasoned veteran of the child-care game.

What had changed my wife's mind in such a short time? Common sense had prevailed. I was busy juggling a full-time job with part-time study commitments and was not available to provide my wife with a regular break so that she could escape to pursue a personal interest.

At that time she was playing indoor cricket and luckily the centre provided creche facilities. She admits to feeling guilty the first time she left our son in the care of strangers. When she returned to find him happily playing, she realised that it was she who was suffering from anxiety attacks, not the baby. Besides, she felt terrific after an energetic game and some adult company.

Relatives make great babysitters, but if they're scarce there are a number of alternatives. You can even have a mutual arrangement with a friend, 'You mind mine and I'll mind yours'. Whatever arrangement you make will pay dividends in terms of recharging those tired batteries.

Mixing with others

Other people give us energy. They can revitalise us and help us get a realistic view of events and our life. Parents tend to mix with other parents. We are drawn to each other like magnets. Put a group of parents in a room for long enough and the conversation will invariably turn to children. It's natural to want to talk to like-minded people, swap information, share stories and seek feedback about your parenting methods.

But they don't all have to be parents. It's also important to mix with people who don't have children. The advantage for parents who work outside the home is that they mix with people who couldn't give a hoot about their child's first steps. The conversation turns to other topics which stimulate the brain in other ways. One of the problems I have encountered with people who have been the primary caregiver is that they often feel a lack self-confidence when in social situations. They've mixed with parents and talked about little else but children's issues for so long that they feel they have little to offer in the conversation stakes. The world has passed them by while they've been raising children.

This isn't true, of course, but it can be a realistic perception for a person who feels out of touch with the wider world. It is essential for our own self-worth that we seek out people who offer more in terms of conversation than child-talk. Join a craft group or take a class in Japanese — anything to stimulate your grey matter and bring you into contact with people who aren't parents.

Seek out positive people

Positive people replenish us; negative people leave us feeling flat and deflated. Surround yourself with friends who have a cheerful outlook. Positive people are optimists who look for the bright side in any situation. If you're surrounded by people who moan and constantly talk down to children, before long you will think the same.

Recently I met an old friend in the supermarket. She told me that she had four children under the age of seven. Her second child was a real trial, and she was convinced that this youngster had been put on this earth to repay her for all the hard times she'd given her parents. I recall that she was a rather wild teenager. After recounting some hair-raising tales about her youngsters that mainly centred around the difficult second child she claimed, 'You know, I wouldn't be dead for quids'. What a terrific attitude!

Encouragement

How do we keep our self-esteem in good working order? What builds up our inner self and provides us with the confidence to tackle new situations, meet new people, take on challenges and cope with the daily problems associated with raising children? Liberal doses of encouragement help build self-confidence and promote positive feelings of self-worth.

It's easy for parents to become discouraged, particularly if they are isolated from other people or are raising children on their own. Many mothers and fathers have doubts about their abilities as parents. They need reassurance and positive feedback about how they're doing as parents.

It's easy to feel you're not a good parent. Before starting a family many parents have high aspirations, both for themselves and their children. I was certain that my kids would never misbehave and that they would be angels in public. I resolved that I would never chastise my kids in public, and certainly never in anger. I assumed that I would always be in control. I have learned through experience that reality is in fact quite different. There are many unforeseen difficulties in parenting.

Positive feedback for parents is essential. Raising children is a combination of so many skills that cannot be mastered immediately, and becoming a good parent takes time and a great deal of trial and error. It's little wonder that many first-borns claim they were experiments for their parents. They were the trailblazers who made the path easier for the siblings who followed.

Spouses and partners, friends and relatives are excellent sources of encouragement. Steer clear of people who criticise or wrap their advice in a thin veil of disapproval. 'I think young Giorgio should start school at four-and-a-half. Why do you want to wait a year?' Such unqualified advice you can do without.

My spouse is a constant source of encouragement whom I can go to regularly when self-doubts arise. However, there are times when other people are more appropriate for offering encouragement. When I assumed the role of primary caregiver in my family I received great support from my spouse, and terrific feedback from my friends who constantly reassured me that many of the decisions I made about childrearing were well-intentioned and had a modicum of common sense.

Kids can be a great source of encouragement. Not only can we take great heart in their personal successes and triumphs but they can actively encourage us with their words. Displays of appreciation for meals cooked or time spent with them do wonders for our self-worth. However, children need to be taught encouragement. They learn this skill primarily from us. If we show appreciation for their help around the house, take pleasure from their triumphs, display confidence in them and concentrate on their strengths, they will learn to both encourage themselves and build up the self-worth of others around them.

Self-encouragement
I'm okay, you're okay
If those around you don't encourage you, turn to the one person whom you can rely on — yourself. Self-encouragement results from positive self-talk and taking pride in your accomplishments. There has been a great deal

written about the benefits of positive self-talk. Basically, self-talk is a personal message to ourselves which both reflects and creates our attitude.

If I tell myself often enough that I'm useless at music, then I'm reflecting and reinforcing a belief about my musical abilities, so that the likelihood of suddenly taking up trombone lessons will be met with a 'Don't be silly. I can't learn an instrument'. If, however, I constantly tell myself that I'm good at music, I am reinforcing and in fact creating a positive view of myself.

Let's relate this back to the parenting role. If we send positive messages to ourselves, then we will not only believe them but act in ways that reinforce that positive attitude. Tell yourself constantly that you are doing a good job, that parenting is a worthwhile task requiring a myriad of skills, that you are willing to try different techniques, and that failure is an invitation to try again.

Reinforce these views daily, even if it means mouthing the words in the mirror each morning. Create your own 'I'm okay' feeling by keeping a realistic attitude, seeking out positive people and taking pleasure in your own accomplishments and those of your children — no matter how small.

Chapter 3

MAINTAINING YOURSELF AS A PERSON

We all have three important areas of our life which we must constantly balance — family, friends and work. For adults who raise children full time, the line between work and family becomes a little hazy. The proportion of time and energy devoted to each fluctuates. For many parents, particularly those with very young children, the family becomes the focus at the expense of other areas.

Raising children can be frustrating for parents who have placed careers on hold. They may even resent the intrusion of kids in their lives and lament that the world is passing them by. Many participants in the training seminars I have given for parents returning to the workforce devalued the skills they acquired from their parenting experiences. On reflection, they realised that the role of parent and all the accompanying tasks had given them new dimensions and skills.

As mothers (most of the seminar attendees were women), they had practised communication skills on a daily basis in trying circumstances and had learned tolerance and patience, which are essential in many jobs. Many remarked how well organised they had been forced to become. Others remarked on their newly acquired time–management skills as they juggled busy schedules around their children's needs.

The task of parenting is so often underestimated, particularly by parents themselves. It's a difficult job which requires so many skills that can be utilised in other areas of endeavour.

Develop personal interests

Personal hobbies revitalise us. Many parents neglect to maintain or develop interests or hobbies. Working parents are often so busy juggling family duties and keeping their employer satisfied that they forget to set aside personal time. Non-working parents often take on extra interests, yet a lot of these activities revolve around children, such as joining school committees or coaching sport teams. This is great, as children benefit greatly from parents' interest and involvement, but they also benefit from parents who can develop their own interests and pursue their own hobbies.

Hobbies are more than a mere diversion from the normal daily grind; they put our lives into perspective. We need to allow ourselves time to refill the tank.

Hobbies can give us self-confidence. A few years ago a friend with three young children recalled her nervousness about accompanying her husband to a work cocktail party. She was afraid that she would have nothing interesting to talk about. I was puzzled by her confession as she was an outgoing, vivacious woman who was able to put other people at ease when she spoke.

She had spent the last six years raising children, and either spent most of her day talking to children, or mixing with other parents who inevitably talked about children. She felt she had nothing to offer as she had neglected to pursue any interests of her own. Dressmaking was her hobby, but she conceded that most of her time was spent making her children's clothes. Some hobby!

My friend lacked a great deal of self-confidence. Personal interests are an excellent way of building self-confidence. Many mothers complain that they have nothing of interest to talk about. All they can discuss is children. Hobbies help fill that void and provide an outside interest that can add a sparkle to your life.

But I haven't the time or the money . . .

It is not my intention to provide a list of possible interests or activities that parents can pursue. The list would be endless. Look around and see what other people are doing. Think of what you would really like to do if you didn't have kids. Interests can be as passive as joining a local reader's circle or as active as participating in aerobics classes. They can be as cheap as walking with a group of friends or as costly as you wish.

It is essential to make time for yourself. Parents put themselves second to their children so often that they forget to grant themselves permission to come first, occasionally. Forget the excuses and any feelings of guilt you may have. A well-rounded person with personal hobbies is far more interesting to live with than a parent who doesn't extend their personal side.

Getting out of the rut. Not long ago I encountered a mother of two school-aged children who felt she was stuck in a rut and needed to do something about it. Bronwyn held down a part-time job in a supermarket and complained that she spent all her time either at work or looking after her children. She knew that she was becoming increasingly grumpy to live with, so to add some sparkle to her life, she decided to do something that she had always wanted to do — skydiving.

'Don't be silly, mum. You can't do that', her children said. Thanks for the vote of confidence, Bronwyn thought, more determined than ever to do something to change her children's perception of her. After her initial jump she felt exhilarated; she had found something that was hers and hers alone. Skydiving is now her passion, rather than her interest. Her children are thrilled that they can boast to their friends of their mother's new hobby. 'My mother is a skydiver. What does your mum do?'

What are your goals?

We establish all sorts of goals to work towards. We have career goals, savings goals, financial goals and home-improvement goals. We may even help our kids establish study aims and objectives. Plans and good intentions abound. Personal interest goals are often made around New Year and are soon scrapped when they compete with the more important family-oriented goals. As well-intentioned parents we so often place ourselves second for the good of others.

Set realistic goals. The following is a list of goals generated by parents at a seminar I conducted recently: learn a language; join a motorbike club; cross-stitch a quilt; go to Tai Chi classes; ride a bike three times a week; play golf once a week; read for at least half an hour a day; swim on a regular basis; learn jazz ballet; or take tennis lessons to improve their backhand.

Make plans to achieve your goals. This may mean revising your household routine, soliciting the help of your partner or parents, or even employing a babysitter to provide the necessary time off for you to pursue your interests. If this meets with resistance from your partner, encourage him or her to take up a hobby as well, and provide some time off for them too. Some time for yourselves will make you both more interesting and relaxed people to live with.

Partner time

Parents often relate to each other as parents rather than as partners. One of the difficulties of raising children is

finding time to be with your partner. Most of the time partners are together they're surrounded by children, and
when they find time to be alone, conversation can be
dominated by child-related issues. While it's important to
share the joys and problems of bringing up kids, it's also
necessary to remove the parent hat and relate to each
other as people.

**Partner relationships need to be nurtured in
much the same way as they were pre-children.**
Remember the times when you would spend hours in
each other's company, talking about seemingly insignifi-
cant matters which opened windows onto each other's
personalities? Yes, you simply enjoyed each other's company. If such intimate moments are now a distant
memory, consider building some regular partner time into
your life.

A couple I am particularly fond of realised that their
lives had become so busy and complicated that they
barely had any time to themselves. They are dedicated
parents and lead full lives, with personal commitments
that often take one or the other away from home. Their
weekends were invariably spent in the service of their
children, and both felt that they had become glorified taxi-
drivers, as they spent most of their spare time carting
children all over the countryside for Cub camps, ballet
lessons and sporting events.

They felt that their relationship was being held
together by the common bond of raising their children,
and that they needed time together to relate to each other

on an intimate basis. They hired a capable student to take over at home once a week so they could spend some time together. The student organised the usual chores such as preparing the meal, folding washing, supervising baths and helping with homework. My friends used this time as couple time. They would go out for a quick meal, take in a evening movie or simply remain at home, relaxing with a drink away from the pressures of their children.

This not only rekindled their relationship but refreshed them for the task of parenting.

What about my sex life?

If you're reading this book, chances are you're well aware of one of the purposes of sex — procreation. You may be thinking that you have done your bit for the continuation of the species. But don't abandon your love life just yet. Sex is a great form of relaxation, obviously a pleasant form of recreation and a great way of building a relationship with a partner.

Sex can be timetabled, if necessary. Sex is not expensive, can be done in your own home and is a great deal of fun. Sadly, busy parents often neglect their sex life. Complaints of 'I'm too tired' or 'We just don't have the time anymore' are common. Parents often have to work harder to maintain a healthy love life. But the rewards are worth it as sex is something you do for yourself as well as your partner.

Some couples are so busy that their intimate moments have to be timetabled, just as they would place an important meeting in their diary. That's okay — it just means you now have to plan your spontaneity. This is fine if it allows people to get together on a regular basis.

'But what if we get caught by the kids?' Some parents are afraid that they may be caught in a compromising position, or at the wrong moment by unsuspecting children who innocently wander into the bedroom.

Bedroom etiquette

A bedroom is a private place. It is a refuge where both adults and children can relax, play and be on their own. Parents and children need a place to go where they know they won't be disturbed. Establish the following rules with your children, who need to learn that there are limits to certain areas of the house.

- A closed bedroom door, day or night, is a sign that privacy is wanted. Even adults need to respect this.

- Children should knock and wait to be invited into a bedroom. If no one answers then they shouldn't go in, even if they just want to borrow a tennis ball for a game. Respect the privacy of bedrooms.

- Parents need to get into the habit of closing their bedroom door at night to allow intimacy to occur. Most parents have developed the habit of leaving their doors open at night when their children are young, and forget to close it even for a short time as their kids get older.

Partner time-out

'I'll hear the children read while you take a break for half an hour', is an offer too good to refuse. Couples work in a number of ways. Some couples have clearly delineated roles that divide tasks into 'his' and 'hers'. Even in the current era that values diversity, these tasks generally follow traditional roles. Many households are still dominated by the 'that's women's work and this is men's work' routine.

There are couples who share household and parenting tasks evenly. Tasks such as washing clothes, cooking and mowing the lawn are divided on a sensible needs basis rather than by strict sex roles. Couples who communicate their needs and develop a sense of teamwork are also in a position to provide each other with time out. By sharing the load parents can gain some much-earned personal time, even if only for ten minutes.

Sole parents

Sole parents have an even greater need to take a break from their children. Many sole parents get little or no respite, particularly if their kids aren't of school age. It's important for your personal well-being to have a break from your children at least once a week. Kids will not only benefit by having a more relaxed parent but they will appreciate being in the company of someone different. Friends, parents, babysitters or creches can be used to provide sole parents, with a well-earned break (see Support network, page 45, and Chapter 11 for further information and addresses).

Three getaway ideas with your partner

Everyone likes to get away. Hotels and travel agencies advertise a host of getaway packages for couples WITHOUT the kids. They can range from simple weekend retreats in the country to extended breaks in exotic locations. But you don't have to have an expensive holiday to get away. In fact, you can escape in your own home every day. Here are three ideas which will help you to relax, connect with your partner and forget about the rest of the world — even if only for a while.

1 Chat and chew

The hour around mealtime when everyone converges at once can be the hardest time of the day. But it can be a great time if we allow it. When you or your partner come home in the evening, resist going straight into overdrive: cooking, bathing, folding washing or whatever.

Push the work aside for a short time and:

1 Sit down in a comfortable part of the house.

2 Let your kids know that you require some private time for a short period. Plan activities to keep them busy if necessary.

3 Chat with each other or simply sit quietly and enjoy.

4 Chew some nibbles or a snack to keep you going. You may find it needs to be washed down with your favourite drink.

continued

You will now feel more like tackling the evening's activities as you have wound down in a civilised manner — probably in much the same way as you did pre-children.

2 Regular rendezvous

Arrange to meet with your partner on a regular basis to share a cup of coffee, a drink, or even a meal. This should occur outside the house. Change the venue and activity but try to keep the time constant. Diaries are filled with meeting times, doctor's appointments and teacher–parent interview times, but rarely do they include couple time. Place a regular time in your diary or on the calendar so that you arrange appointments around your rendezvous time.

Be firm — do not put your rendezvous off because it's the only time you can get a hair appointment.

How regular? Once a fortnight is great but a monthly basis may be more realistic for some busy couples.

3 One weekend a year

Have one annual weekend without the kids. Book them into their grandparents or make arrangements with friends. You may even mind your friends' kids for a weekend in return so they too can enjoy a weekend alone. You don't have to stay in an expensive hotel, although it is a pleasant option. Stay at home if your budget is stretched, and prepare a special meal, or eat out. Make the effort to make the weekend special for you and your partner.

Plan the weekend well in advance so that you have something to look forward to. And don't talk about the kids!

Support network

'I don't need any help. I can cope quite well, thanks very much.' This is the martyr's catchcry. We all need help and support from time to time. If you're feeling tired or ready to explode if your kids don't cooperate, it's essential to communicate your needs to someone. Tell a spouse, friend, relative or a professional counsellor. Seek out the assistance you need. A sole-parent friend of mine who has raised three children on her own for many years has a favourite saying: 'Martyrs die alone.' Rather dramatic but the message has a ring of truth to it!

Examine your support network.

Who can you go to to talk about any difficulties you may have?

Who can mind the children for a short time while you have a nap or get a little exercise?

Do you have access to a babysitter or creche?

Do you have someone you can go to for a chat or a laugh when you feel down?

Who gives you a boost when you need it most?

Support can come from many different areas. It can be provided by a spouse or partner, friends, relatives or organised agencies such as Infant Welfare Centres (or the equivalent in your state) and local government support groups. Identify members of your support network and ask yourself if they provide three basic functions: babysitting; someone you can share problems with; and someone who can encourage you or make you laugh when you need it.

If any of these three areas are neglected then make plans to rectify the situation. If friends or relatives are scarce then seek assistance through organised groups or agencies. Many organisations and activity groups offer free or inexpensive childcare facilities. Most towns and suburbs have babysitting clubs where members mind each other's children either during the day or in the evenings. There is no need to isolate yourself as help and assistance are available. Most of the support and networks that you need should be available at a local level.

Local or shire council

The local council or shire is an excellent starting point for parents who need assistance of any type. If the local government doesn't offer the service you need they should be able to refer you to someone who can.

Collect a shire or council booklet which outlines the services, hobby and interest groups which operate in the area.

Citizens Advice Bureaus

These are located throughout Australia with the purpose of advising the community of the services available in an area.

Community or neighbourhood houses

Community houses are located in most areas and offer a variety of cheap, interesting programs and activities for community members (both parents and kids) during the day and at night. They often have free childcare as well.

Community Maternal and Child Health Centres (Infant Welfare Centres)

These centres offer practical assistance, support and advice for parents of children under six. They are also an excellent resource for what is available in the local community. A good Maternal and Child Health nurse is worth her weight in gold. Not only can she put you in touch with any organisations you might require, but can help you make contact with other parents in the community.

Playgroups

Playgroups are not just for the kids! They operate in most towns and provide the opportunity for toddlers and babies (and their parents) to interact and socialise once or twice a week. Contact your local government or your Maternal and Child Health nurse for details.

Occasional Care

This facility is available throughout Australia, usually through child care centres, and provides parents of children under the age of six with a break. This is just the thing for tired parents who need relief from their kids. Contact your local Maternal and Child Health nurse or the local council for your nearest child care centre which offers occasional care.

Before- and after-school care

Many schools have subsidised before- and after-school care for their students which can be used on an occasional basis to provide parents with a break. For more information contact your children's school.

(One couple I know leave their two primary children in after-school care while they go swimming once a week. The kids love it and their parents are able to exercise while spending time together.)

Sporting and hobby clubs

Many health-and-fitness and sport centres offer free childcare for participants. Sure, you may have to pay for the session, but babysitting is a bonus. Some sporting groups which play during the day, such as tennis and netball clubs, offer free or cheap childcare.

You stay home and your child goes out

As children become more independent you may consider that they share an activity, thus giving you a short break to do as you wish. Music lessons, ballet, Cubs, sport — take your pick. Share the driving with a friend so that you don't spend all the time in the car.

Babysitting clubs

Babysitting clubs offer parents the chance to have a night out without the kids. They usually have reciprocal babysitting arrangements. That is, you mind other children in exchange for yours being minded. If there isn't one in your area consider starting your own with parents at playgroup, kindergarten or school.

For special support
Nursing Mothers Association of Australia

Victoria (03) 9885 0855

Queensland (07) 3844 6488

New South Wales (02) 9686 4141

ACT (02) 6258 8928

Tasmania (03) 6331 2799

South Australia (08) 8411 0050

Western Australia (08) 9309 5393

Northern Territory (08) 8981 7086

Parents in any state or territory should contact the Victorian (national headquarters) office if they experience any difficulty contacting a voluntary counsellor.

You can also visit their website at www.nmaa.asn.au for further information.

Australian Multiple Births Association (Twins Club)

The AMBA is a volunteer group which operates nationally to provide advice and practical assistance to parents of twins and other multiple births. They also provide social opportunities for parents as well. Contact Australian Multiple Births Association, PO Box 105, Coogee, NSW 2034 for the Twins Club nearest to you.

You can also contact your local GP or church. For sole parents there is a list of support groups in Chapter 11 (see pages 169–70).

Chapter 4

MY PARTNER HAS A DIFFERENT APPROACH FROM ME

'I wish my partner could hear what you say about discipline. He would change his mind.'

'The children's father is far too strict, particularly on our eldest son.'

'My wife gives in too easily to the kids. One only has to throw a tantrum and she's willing to hand over the family heirlooms for a bit of peace.'

'Tom is always spoiling for a fight. He flies off the handle when the children disagree with him. If only he'd talk things through.'

What these people are really saying is, 'As a parent I wish my partner was more like me'. Differences in parenting approaches are quite natural, and are often raised at parenting seminars. Differences are healthy, a sign of independent thinking, and can provide a sense of balance to family life.

The important issue is how the variations in approach are handled by both parents and the effect this approach can have on children and parents themselves. Different approaches can cause discomfort, stress and anxiety to one or both parents, especially if the variation is significant.

How do partners differ?
Discipline
Different approaches to discipline are the source of greatest parental concern. Often one parent may be too strict while the other is far too lenient. In the vernacular of one parent, 'Their father is as tough as nails and he reckons I let them get away with murder. I think I'm being reasonable'. The clash between authoritarian, dominant approaches and a democratic approach, which allows children a degree of freedom, is usually at the heart of these differences.

Punishment can often vary between parents. One may believe the old adage of 'spare the rod and spoil the child' while the other parent prefers to reason with children and use behavioural consequences to promote responsibility for their actions. Discipline differences are usually revealed over specific issues such as swearing, lying or teenagers going out.

A mother recently described her horror when her husband washed her nine-year-old daughter's mouth out with soap and water after he heard her swearing. He had rarely physically punished her before so she was surprised by both the nature and the intensity of his reaction. He obviously held a strong belief about swearing and acted accordingly. Certain behaviours and incidents can trigger surprising parental reactions.

Who's in charge?

Partners have different beliefs about managing family life. This often results in a dispute over family leadership. Dad may believe that he should be in charge of the family, just as his father was. Accordingly, he believes that it's his role to make most of the family decisions and administer justice when needed. Mum may resent this dominance and believe that not only should she have a greater say in the running of the family but that the kids should have a greater voice in their own affairs and in the family life. Differences in beliefs may result in overt conflict between parents or in one giving in to the demands of the other to maintain peace.

Giving in is a common approach. The amount of responsibility given to children demonstrates differences in beliefs and attitudes about childrearing. Fiona, a mother of three primary-school children, gave a great deal of responsibility to her kids for their own basic welfare, including getting themselves up and ready for school in the morning, packing their own lunches and leaving for school on time. She believed that she was teaching children independence by adopting a passive role, particularly in the morning.

Robert, her husband, was an only child whose mother performed most of these tasks and more for him as a child. He firmly believed that kids needed to be pampered, and that they should enjoy being children and not be burdened with excessive chores and responsibilities. 'There will be enough time later on for them to develop independence. Why rush it?'

Fiona and Robert had such diverse views on child-raising and the roles that parents should take in kids' development that they had many heated arguments. As the children grew older these differences were more pronounced. Robert believed his influence was less obvious as Fiona had assumed the role of main caregiver. Over time he had handed most of the responsibility to his wife. Robert thought that by staying out of it not only would he reduce conflict but that Fiona would take full responsibility for any problems that may arise as a result of her approach to raising children.

One partner giving in to the other is a common solution to the differences that can occur between parents. Further on we shall explore some approaches that couples like Robert and Fiona might take in the search for some common ground.

'But dad says I can!' — different standards

'You shouldn't let them speak to you like that. If they

argue like that with me I'll soon set them straight.' We all have different expectations about behaviour which often result from our own upbringing. What is an acceptable standard of behaviour for one parent may be totally unacceptable to another. Children learn about these different parental standards early on. They may argue with mum to get their own way or to gain a little ground but they would not dare question their father's authority as he would see this as akin to mutiny. So they behave and react to their parents accordingly.

Kids recognise differences in standards. Mum may insist that they eat every scrap on their plate while dad doesn't mind if some food is left for the dog. Such matters may appear rather superficial, but they can be infuriating for parents who feel that they are not being supported by their partner. As an exasperated mother claimed, 'I spend so much time teaching my children good manners and my husband couldn't care less if they said please or not. All my good work just goes out the window.'

Solving disputes

My way is the right way. Parents differ in the way they handle family conflict. Some believe in no conflict at all while others believe that conflict is not only normal but a sign of a health family. Look at the many ways people deal with disagreements and differences of opinion. Some will avoid it at all costs; some will retreat after a brief confrontation and allow conflict to simmer; some like to deal with conflict on the spot; and some tend to quietly talk through disputes and search for a solution that pleases everyone; others refuse to budge. No matter how we deal with conflict, we all tend to instinctively feel that our way is correct.

I thought we agreed on this

Most people choose a long-term partner thinking he or she is similar. The honeymoon period soon stops as partners discover differences over what time to get up in the morning, what time dinner should be served and, indeed, who should cook dinner. As time goes on these significant differences reveal individual values. These differences are usually okay until children arrive on the scene.

Before examining how some of these differences can be handled by partners, it's useful to look at the origin of these different ideas and approaches to parenting, and the way we relate to others.

Why are there differences?

Voices from the past

We are shaped by our own family experiences. Not only do we learn the physical aspects of child-rearing, such as feeding babies and comforting sick children, from our own parents, but we use our own parents as a reference point when dealing with the whole range of issues that affect family life. Our experiences of family life are reflected in the way we relate to our children, our expectations of them, our beliefs about child-rearing and the atmosphere we establish in our family.

We are influenced by our own place in our original family. The youngest child in a family of four will certainly have a different perspective on how a family should conduct itself than the eldest. Both children will carry these views into their own families which will help determine how they relate to their spouses and rear their children. The eldest may be authoritarian by nature and have high expectations for his own children, just as his parents had for him. The youngest, however, may believe that his children should receive all they want, just as he did as a child.

Glenn and Rhonda: a case study

Glenn came from a large, boisterous family which valued open, frank discussion. Arguments between siblings were frequent, rarely intense and quickly forgotten. Both parents were extremely affectionate. It was still the custom for Glenn to greet his now adult siblings with a kiss or a hug.

Rhonda, his partner, was drawn to his demonstrative manner, and was envious of the intensity which dominated the family's relationships and the atmosphere of acceptance. Everyone had a positive outlook and encouraged each other at every opportunity. They seemed to grasp life with so much passion that Rhonda felt a little intimidated. She wanted so much for her family life to be like Glenn's.

Rhonda's family was quite different. She was the elder of two sisters and her father had separated from her

continued

mother when she was eight. Her mother became increasingly distant, and there were many communication barriers as several subjects were taboo. Rhonda's mother became extremely critical of the two sisters, and nothing was ever good enough, whether it be their school marks or their friends. Rhonda put up with her mother's criticisms and learned to keep to herself. Even as a teenager she complied with her mother's wishes in an effort to avoid upsetting her.

Glenn and Rhonda approached parenting differently. As much as she wanted to be like her spouse, Rhonda found that her family values reflected those she had experienced as a child — the very ideals she thought she'd rejected. Rhonda also tried to make Glenn more like her, as a parent.

As Rhonda had high expectations of her children she would constantly point out their deficiencies so they could improve, whereas Glenn was more accepting and was dismayed by his wife's constant criticism. Glenn was a very loving father who expressed his affection openly. Rhonda found it difficult to be affectionate to her children, particularly in public. She also found it difficult to express her emotions and encouraged her youngsters to hide their feelings. She praised them if they didn't cry and expected them to show restraint when they were happy. Glenn would cry at weddings as well as at funerals and couldn't help letting the whole world know when one of his children had done well at school or in sport.

> Rhonda and Glenn have raised three happy children who are now well-adjusted adults. They each adapted to the other, despite their different families of origin.

Learned parental sexism. 'Little girls shouldn't play such rough games. You're not a boy, you know,' said Terrence to his four-year-old daughter. His wife couldn't believe what she'd just heard. 'Where did you get an attitude like that? Little girls shouldn't play rough games! How should they play then?' she asked. Terrence was surprised at what he'd said. He'd considered himself to be a forward-thinking male who was trying to break down sexual stereotypes for his children, yet he had blurted out a statement like that.

Terrence was reflecting his own parents' attitude to sex roles which was strongly ingrained in his psyche. Like Terrence, we hold strong beliefs and attitudes that reflect those of our parents. As they were our most significant models for our formative years, the lessons we learn from them often reappear years later when we become parents.

You're just like your mother

Now where did you learn that? When we're under stress we tend to respond to conflict in the same way as we learned in our original family. We may learn to handle conflict in new, rationally applied ways, however, when the pressure is on and emotional control is tested, we tend to revert to our old ways. Explore your own way of dealing with conflict and look closely at your reaction when there is a disagreement.

Do you

a give in to keep the peace?

b avoid conflict but just do as you wish anyway?

c sulk, which is really a silent temper tantrum?

d aggressively argue and stick up for your views?

e seek a solution that satisfies both?

f want the other person to come around to your way of thinking?

When you have worked out your usual reaction to conflict, identify those people in your original family who used the same tactics when conflict occurred.

The influence of your parents

Use these questions to help you revisit your own family and gain a greater understanding of the way you act as a parent. Try to recall or imagine how your parents would have handled these situations. Ask your partner to do the same and use the results to stimulate discussion about your similarities and differences. You can add to the list of areas to be explored.

Fun

What did your parents do together? How did they have fun with their children?

Parenting practices
How did they act as parents? Were they affectionate, loud, silent, fair? What did you like about them? What did you dislike?

Discipline
Describe the discipline in your home as a child. Who was responsible for discipline?

Decision-making
Who made the important decisions? How were decisions generally reached?

Sex roles
Were girls and boys treated differently? If so, how? Were the expectations about school and jobs different?

Education
How was education viewed? Was it important?

Conflict
How was conflict handled? What approaches were used by parents?

Chores
Were you expected to do chores? If so, what types? What happened if they were not done?

Family meals
What kind of atmosphere was there at mealtimes? What kind a rituals were there at mealtime? Were mealtimes pleasant experiences?
continued

Training methods

How much responsibility were you given as a child? What types of responsibility were you given?

Conclusion

Which experiences or practices do you wish to repeat with your family?

Dealing with the differences

Partners who have different parenting approaches are not abnormal. It's healthy to expose children to a variety of ideas about a range of matters. In many cases parents can complement each other. Different strengths, preferences and approaches can be a tremendous asset to any family. It's not parental differences that present problems, it's how they're dealt with.

Identify the major differences between partners. Examine your personal strengths and weaknesses, your values and beliefs about parenting, your expectations for your children and standards of behaviour, and methods of dealing with family conflict. Use the parent activity on pages 60–2 as a guide to re-examining your parenting approaches. Compare yourself with your partner. Gain an understanding of your partner's views from his or her perspective. When you have identified the major differences between you, you can then work out how to deal with them, together or individually.

Compromise — finding a common ground

Compromise is often seen as a dirty word. It can be misconstrued as giving in to the other side. Compromise is really the art of finding common ground and searching for a solution which both parties can live with. It is sometimes known as finding a 'win–win' situation. Parents often compromise with each other on a regular basis without being aware of it.

Alex and Nola, parents of three school-aged children, disagreed over their kids' dress standards. Alex thought that they dressed poorly, particularly for school, while Nola believed that they should be free to make their own clothing decisions. Conflict arose when Alex tried to pressure the children to wear a school uniform and they turned to their mother for support. A sticky situation!

Alex and Nola tried to see the situation from each other's perspective. They decided to compromise. Nola agreed that there should be reasonable dress standards for special occasions such as school. Alex agreed to allow his children to choose leisure clothes, and promised not to comment on their choices. Together, he and Nola were now able to present a united front to their children on the issue of dressing.

But we need consistent rules

Imagine driving a car if there were two sets of road rules. Unthinkable! There would be accidents in the first five minutes. Similarly, there would be chaos in a family if there were more than one set of rules. While acceptance of behaviour standards may vary within a partnership, the rules that govern family living need to be agreed upon. These rules, which govern a range of issues from bedtime to household tidiness, must be known and consistently applied or there will be confusion.

Keeping out

When a partner feels strongly about a certain discipline issue or method of raising children, it is wise to allow that person to handle that area. Robert, who disagreed with the way Fiona handled the morning routine, was sensible enough to allow his wife to organise that time of the day. Fiona felt strongly about encouraging independence in her youngsters and saw the mornings as the perfect vehicle.

Robert accepted this, stayed out of the way in the morning and exerted his influence in other ways or at more appropriate times.

Family meetings

Some parents have found that the regular use of family meetings is a pragmatic way to reach a common approach as well as providing a forum for resolving some family disputes. Regular family meetings are not for everyone, but they offer a structured approach to help parents get on the same wavelength. However, both parents must be willing partners in the enterprise if they are to be successful.

What is a meeting for?

1 Allocating chores.

2 Conflict resolution and providing assistance with individual problems.

3 Establishing rules, procedures and routines.

4 Planning enjoyable activities.

How can we make a meeting work?

Family meetings are most successful when held on a weekly or fortnightly basis. They require a simple agenda to keep the meeting on track. The agenda can consist of the following items:

1 *Encouragement.* Each member can offer encouraging words to others in the family. (When starting out, parents can provide a strong lead in this area.)

2 *Issues to be discussed.* No more than two or three issues should be discussed. Issues can come from children or adults. It's helpful to have an agenda pinned to the fridge which can be added to as the need arises.

3 *Finances.* This is a good time to provide children with any pocket money they may receive.

4 *Enjoyable activity.* Conclude with an enjoyable activity such as a game or story.

continued

As with all meetings, there needs to be a chairperson and a set of rules. At first, parents will need to act as chairpersons, but as children gain in experience this role can be shared around. Simple rules which establish guidelines for the kids need to be made clear from the start.

'We have a problem with . . .' Be careful not to allow the meetings to generate into gripe sessions, which will quickly turn you and the children away. Problems are best presented in non-accusatory language. 'We have a problem with . . .' is a far more conciliatory approach than 'You children never . . .' Try to keep the meetings light and moving reasonably quickly. Fifteen to twenty minutes should be more than enough time.

A united front

There are problems which arise in families where parents need to set aside any differences and take a united front. Some of the issues involving teenagers require careful handling, and differences in parental views and approaches can often lead to confusion, and at times only exacerbate a problem.

Parents need to find common ground when dealing with such issues as alcohol use, parties and sexuality. At such times parents must start talking (if they aren't already doing so), and adopt a consistent approach if they are to guide their adolescent children through these and other real-life issues. When parents have separated a common approach can still be used if both partners are willing to put their differences aside and make decisions with the best interests of their children in mind.

With all due respect

The key to dealing with parental differences is mutual respect. Identify the differences, seek a compromise and learn to handle areas where compromise is not possible. In the following points I have identified common trouble spots.

1 Avoid disagreeing openly with your partner about child-rearing or discipline matters in front of the children. However, when children's health, safety or physical well-being is at risk due to one parent's approach to discipline, then do not hesitate to interfere in whatever way you feel is necessary.

2 Stay out of disputes between your partner and a child.

3 Communicate your concerns to your partner. At times a parent will have strong concerns about the way their partner handles an issue. It is appropriate to discuss these concerns and generate alternative strategies.

4 Avoid overcompensating for a partner. It's better to be consistent, and assist kids in coping with any extreme methods of parenting they may experience, rather than go to the other extreme to make it up to them. Ensure children are exposed to at least one consistent, balanced parenting approach.

5 Have faith in your own influence over your kids, and your ability as a parent to influence children's behaviour, regardless of whether it's supported. I am constantly surprised by the influence a great idea or strategy has on children, even if it isn't supported by a partner.

A final word

Consistency is the real challenge for parents. Differences in parental approaches can be a source of needless worry for parents. While similarity in approaches is desirable, in reality it's often impossible to achieve. It is more important to be consistent so that children can predict your reaction to their misbehaviour, understand your behaviour standards and feel comfortable with you as a person.

Chapter 5

DEALING WITH
MISBEHAVIOUR

'

'What a day!' says Marian to her husband Sam as she crashes into a chair. 'I've spent all day dealing with naughty children. Telling them to do this and not to do that. I don't want to be a policewoman. I want to be a mother.' Expecting to hear an account of a major catastrophe, Sam was surprised when Marian reeled off a litany of minor disturbances that kept her busy for what seemed most of the day.

It's common for parents to feel worn down dealing with kids' misbehaviour. Handling argumentative children, fighting, mealtime misbehaviour and constant interruptions are extremely tiresome. At the end of the day parents may feel worn out, yet nothing major has happened. It's the smaller misdemeanours rather than major behavioural problems which drain parents and leave them irritable. The 'Oh, no, I think I've bred a monster' variety of misbehaviour is rare compared to the smaller, everyday, household kind.

Shouldn't raising children be exciting and rewarding? Yes, but how do you do it without being continually exhausted? The solution to dealing with misbehaviour is in the way parents react. Too often children misbehave and parents react haphazardly. They search through parenting books or seek advice from friends and relatives for solutions to problem behaviours and are disappointed when the strategies don't work.

The overall approach is more crucial than grasping at good ideas. Don't misunderstand me. Good ideas are extremely helpful but they need to be used within a consistent approach to discipline to be really effective.

Do you view discipline as a negative aspect of parenting? This seems to be the view of many people I deal with as a parent educator. Discipline is usually not discussed when planning for a family and is ignored until behavioural problems arise. In fact, it is often narrowly defined as punishment. It derives from the Latin term meaning 'instruction'. Discipline is a teaching function rather than something you must do when kids don't follow rules.

Parents and educators should teach children appropriate ways of behaving in a social context. We are all social beings and as such operate within a set of rules established to maintain our safety and well-being and to protect our own rights, as well as those of others. A family rule stating children should be home by dark is for both children's protection and organisational purposes. An infraction of such a rule needs to be dealt with to teach a child to behave appropriately and remind him of his responsibility to himself and others.

Discipline is all about teaching rather than reacting to behaviour. It is both an active and useful process, rather than a negative, reactionary one. As with all training and teaching, we can predict events and plan effectively to deal consistently with problems.

Wait until your father gets home

In families where the father was the breadwinner and mother was the homemaker the disciplinarian role was traditionally assigned to the male of the house, presumably because he gave a heavier wallop. Mother would deal with the regular misbehaviour and father would dish out punishment for the more serious stuff or when a youngster needed to be taught a lesson.

Discipline is most effective if shared by both partners. The shape of families has changed significantly, whether the two parents are working or the dad stays at home while the mum goes out to work. And there is now a more even spread of roles. It's unreasonable for one parent to be painted as the ogre who dishes out the discipline all the time.

Most misbehaviour reflects a lack of cooperation between two people, so it's up to those two people to sort out the problem. It's more useful for the person whom the misbehaviour affects to deal with that behaviour. Of course, the other partner's support is important if strategies are to be successful.

Develop a discipline plan

As most misbehaviour is minor, it's possible to develop a planned approach to discipline. Preparation and planning help to conserve your mental energy. Anticipation can also prevent situations from occurring or behaviours from escalating. A discipline plan also allows parents to place the responsibility for misbehaving where it belongs — with the child. Consistent, planned responses help children to develop self-discipline as they can think ahead of the likely consequences. Self-control comes when children can readily predict the consequences of their actions.

What about misbehaviour?

Some observations

1 All children misbehave at some stage. They're often testing their limits and wanting to know where the boundaries lie.

2 Often children's misbehaviour is at it's worst when we want it to be at its best. Children need to learn that they must comply with the needs of a given situation, as this is part of living in a social context. Teaching children how to cooperate with others is part of the discipline process.

3 Constant misbehaviour (as in temper tantrums) has the purpose of involving parents and/or teachers. It's usually for the benefit of gaining attention, keeping adults in their service or defeating them. The majority of children's misbehaviours are minor and for the purpose of gaining attention. Parents need to stop paying so much attention to misbehaviour and provide positive responses to cooperative ways of acting. Train yourself to 'catch children being good'.

4 Certain behaviour can bring a strong reaction from one parent while hardly eliciting a murmur from the other. My youngest daughter knows I can't resist any request when she begins that fatal phrase, 'Daddy, can I have . . .', whereas this doesn't wash with her mother.

Similarly, my children realise that whining drives me around the twist, yet it doesn't have quite the same effect on their mother. Through our reactions to children's misbehaviour we often unknowingly encourage it to continue. Children will adopt a behaviour if it's to their advantage.

5 Most misbehaviour is predictable. We can make planned responses rather than rely on impulsive reactions which are high on impact but low on effectiveness.

When developing a planned approach to discipline it's helpful to consider a child's age and temperament and your own capacity to deal with various situations. Let's face it, we cope better on some days than others (as do children), so take this into account. An inflexible way of dealing with children can add to our stress rather than relieve it.

What it involves

1 Establish rules, procedures and reasonable expectations

It's important that family rules and your expectations of children's behaviour are clearly and positively expressed for kids in terms they understand.

'We say please and thank you when we want something' is more meaningfull than 'Use your manners when you want something'. A string of negative rules beginning with 'Don't' tells children what they shouldn't do, but gives little guidance as to what they should be doing.

Children can help to formulate the many procedures and rules that exist in the family. This is smart management as they are more likely to stick to rules that they've had a say in making.

2 Define clear limits

Rules teach children about appropriate behaviour and limits define the boundaries of their activity. Be specific about how you expect children to behave. Outline expected behaviour in specific and clear terms. 'Please play quietly in another area of the house when we visit Jenny' is far more meaningful than 'I want you to be good while we are visiting'.

Children of all ages will push parental boundaries to some extent. They like to test the extremities of these boundaries (and your patience) so you need to have a firm backbone to resist their tantrums, whining and general objections. One British study found that children will push parental boundaries one in three times. That makes limit-setting hard work for parents and suggests that they involve children in the process of setting limits as much as humanly possible.

Avoid grey areas when setting limits. 'Don't be late home' can easily be interpreted by kids to suit themselves. 'But eight o'clock is not late, mum.'

'I meant that you should be home before dark.'

'Well, why didn't you say that?'

The youngster is right. Limits need to be clearly expressed to children of all ages.

3 Remind them only once

It's reasonable in some cases to provide children with a reminder or warning about their behaviour. Young children can have difficulty understanding rules and limits and need to be reminded of appropriate ways of acting. Directions such as John, you're making far too much noise inside' and 'Penny, you're interrupting me while I'm on the phone. Please play a game to keep busy', bring inappropriate behaviour to children's attention. The onus is on them to change.

'Conrad, If you don't clean your teeth you won't have any ice-cream for a month' Avoid making threats you can't carry out. Kids are experts at seeing through such threats and are more likely to comply with reasonable warnings. Besides, it's difficult to build a culture of cooperation in a home where intimidation is used as a tactic.

4 Impose a consequence

Behavioural consequences are a powerful way of teaching children about appropriate behaviour. There are two types of consequences: natural and logical. The former are inherent in the natural order of the environment. A child who refuses to eat his dinner will be hungry, or if he teases a dog he will be bitten. There is little need for adult interference as he will learn through experience how to change his behaviour accordingly.

Logical consequences are used more frequently when behaviour infringes on the rights of others. Their use teaches children to respect order and the rights of others. Consequences are not to be confused with punishment which relies on high impact for much of its effectiveness, and is used as a deterrent.

Behavioural consequences teach children to take responsibility for their behaviour by utilising the three Rs: **related**, **reasonable** and **respectful**. A consequence should be related to a behaviour so that a child clearly associates a misbehaviour with its outcome. Resentment is minimised when consequences are **reasonable** and dignity is maintained when they are **respectful** to the child.

The child who makes a mess in the toilet will learn to

take greater care (and aim) if he is required to clean up after himself. This Is **related** to his action, **reasonable** and **respectful**. It would lead to resentment if he has to clean the kitchen floor as well 'to teach him a lesson'.

Behavioural consequences are most effective when they are delivered calmly. Remember that it's action rather than talk that teaches children about behaviour, so forget the verbal tirade. This is usually for the benefit of parents, not children. The application of consequences requires thought and practice, and a belief that children are capable of regulating their own behaviour.

5 **After the consequence**

A friendly approach following a consequence is welcomed by children. Reassure them that while you disapprove of their behaviour, you still love them. It's important to separate the deed from the doer. It may be useful to spend some time redirecting a child's attention to more useful behaviours, or even invite the child to join you in an activity.

Fighting between siblings

A planned approach to discipline is best demonstrated by dealing with the following common misbehaviours that wear parents out. In each situation the rules and limits have been discussed and are reasonably well understood. Each scenario use consequences to teach children to accept responsibility for their actions. Talk is used to help resolve a problem or conflict, to provide a direction or to remind children about their behaviour.

What do you do when your children fight and argue with each other? Chances are you either plead for peace and quiet, make a ruling to end the dispute, maintain some form of order, or take sides to lay blame on the child who caused the infraction. It is very difficult not to become involved in children's fighting. Look at the nature of most disputes. They generally evolve from a disagreement over some minor issue such as the choice of television programs, the result of a game or a refusal to share a toy. I have witnessed fights in my house over who should sit in a certain chair in the living room. Earth-shattering stuff! The issues may be minor but the results in terms of disturbing peace and tranquillity can be enormous and extremely hard for parents to deal with.

Stages of the fights. Fights usually go through a number of predictable phases. The first is the quiet stage. The dispute then enters phase two as the noise level rises. Kids become agitated and belligerent. The fight is now almost in full swing. Parents need to brace themselves for stage three which is the moving phase. The fight can shift from one area of the house to another. Typical behaviours at this stage are hurling of verbal abuse or insults, shouting, door slamming and hitting or punching.

By this stage it is necessary for a parent to reach for the Walkman or turn up the volume of the television if they want to ignore the fight. You can recognise the final stage as one or all of the parties involved in the fight will come to you crying, pointing the finger at other siblings or with a plea for justice: 'Mum, Carrie hit me and I didn't do anything.'

What do you do now? Take sides with the injured party, bury your head in the sand and hope the whole fight will dissolve, or send them all to their rooms until they have calmed down? It is necessary to have some planned strategies that will not only help children resolve their own dispute but ensure their frequency decreases. It's the noise level and frequency of the fighting that is so draining on parents' energy levels.

Why are my kids fighting with each other?

1 Sibling fighting is common but not necessarily normal behaviour. My research indicates that sibling fighting is a concern to parents in three out of every four families. Children don't have to fight. There is an alternative to energy-sapping, nerve-shattering fighting.

2 Arguing and fighting generally involves parents at some stage in the dispute.

3 A certain amount of conflict is healthy in a family. Children will always have issues and problems that need to be dealt with or resolved. Conflict can be dealt with so there are no losers, and no arguing and punching. Teach children to compromise so that both parties in a dispute feel as if they have achieved something. It is possible to have a 'win-win' situation in most disputes.

4 Children are capable of resolving their disputes amicably. They may need guidance and assistance, though, particularly when they are younger. Fighting between

siblings may not be eradicated but it certainly can be reduced and, importantly, its effect on parents can be minimised.

Dealing with the disputes

There are two broad approaches that parents can adopt with sibling fighting. Parents can choose to become involved or they can remain neutral.

The approach you take will depend on many factors such as the age, maturity and ability of the children to sort out their own problems, your ability to ignore noise and your beliefs about how conflict should be resolved.

Getting involved

1 **Intervene early.** It's easier to sort out a problem before a fullscale fight occurs. Otherwise, you have two issues to sort out — the fight and the original problem.

2 **Help children resolve their problem rather than the dispute.** Let them know that you're willing to help them resolve the issues that sparked the dispute, but are unwilling to take sides. Establish what the fight or argument is about and offer suggestions to resolve the issue.

3 **Discuss alternatives to fighting.** It takes two or more to fight or argue. Even so-called victims can protect themselves. When a dispute occurs they can go to a bedroom or even move close to you if safety is an issue. Teach children how to discuss issues quietly rather than

through shouting or attempting to win. It may be helpful to set aside a regular time each week to discuss issues of concern.

4 **Establish limits and rules for resolving disputes.** If children are to fight then they should do it in a way and place that least disturbs you. A father who established the simple rule that noisy fights were okay if waged outside, found that the incidence of fighting reduced dramatically. His youngsters never fought with each other after dark.

5 **Help children move on.** Some children need assistance to close their disputes with siblings. It helps sometimes when a dispute has run its course to insist that they end the dispute and move on. They may not have to 'kiss and make up' but a hug is a good way of inviting them to move on and put the conflict behind them. The most important thing for children following a dispute is to get on with constructive, pro-social activities whether they involve a sibling or not. It is the fights that go on and on or just simmer away that can be so destructive to family harmony.

Children learn the rules of fighting and settling disagreements in a healthy, well-functioning family. The challenge for parents is to provide kids with the space and the tools to resolve issues for themselves. Sometimes they do so by themselves and sometimes they require a little adult help.

Staying out of it

A refusal to enter children's fights is not a capitulation or an act of avoidance. Parents who believe that children are capable of resolving most of their own disputes are displaying tremendous faith, and placing responsibility where it should lie. Fighting usually decreases when parents refuse to enter into children's disputes. So when children fight you can make one of three choices:

Bear it. If you're able to tune out from noisy behaviour.

Beat it. If you can't resist interfering or just can't stand the noise, go to another part of the house. Try leaving the house if necessary.

Boot them out. Limit fighting to a particular part of the house, or even outside. If they continue to fight inside, then put them out in silence. Your apparent lack of concern has a powerful affect on the incidence of fighting.

Encourage children's efforts to resolve problems amicably. Point out to them any instances where they have listened to each other, discussed a potential problem or reached a compromise. Inform them of what they have done. This is an excellent teaching exercise.

Argumentative children

'Bryce, would you tidy your bedroom, please?'

'Why do I have to? It's my room.'

'I have visitors coming today I would like to have the house tidy, please.'

'But they're not my visitors. They're yours. They won't care how my room looks.'

'Maybe not. But I do.'

Does this sound familiar? Are you tired of every little request being met with an argument or that age-old retort, 'Why?' Often what parents and children argue about is not the real issue. Children often argue to

---

What to do when they argue with you

1 Stop and make eye contact. Ensure that you make eye contact and that the message has been received.

2 Be clear with your instructions. Be specific about what you want done and when it is to be done.

3 Repeat, if necessary, but refuse to enter into a debate. Stay calm, breathe slowly and show that you are unwilling to argue but that you are willing to persist with your request.

4 Move away and give your child time to comply.

5 If your child simply refuses, stay calm and consider a consequence for his non-cooperation. This is not to punish him but to demonstrate the importance of family cooperation. We all benefit when we cooperate. You may consider withdrawing your cooperation temporarily as a consequence.

demonstrate their power — 'You can't make me do anything I don't want to do.' This type of behaviour is
common for firstborns and adolescents. Remember that
you are powerful too and can act in ways that positively
exert your influence. **Refuse to argue with children.** Recognise that an
argument is often an invitation to fight. Sidestep the
dispute. State your request and refuse to be drawn into
an argument. Some children are consummate bush
lawyers and delight in proving you wrong on a minor
point of law. 'You want me to clean my room, huh? Have
you cleaned your room yet?' argues our budding
debater.

The language of choice

'**You may tidy your room either now or before you
have dinner. Please choose.**' Argumentative children,
like all power-hungry children, generally respond readily
when offered choices, rather than being given straight-
out commands.

'**Am I meddling unnecessarily in my child's
affairs?**' Children can at times have a legitimate reason
for arguing. Check the issues before you intervene. Not
so long ago a father revealed how his daughter would
argue with him over the types of clothes he wanted her
to wear. I was astounded to hear that she was fifteen
years old. No wonder she argued with her father, when
he interfered in an area that was clearly within her
domain.

Temper tantrums

Tricia decided that it was time to bring her six-year-old daughter Ella's bedtime forward by half an hour, as it was obvious she was getting overtired in the evenings. Ella lived an extremely busy life and was coming home from school and lying listlessly on the couch. She was not coping well at all.

When Tricia announced that her bedtime would now be earlier, Ella burst into tears and flung herself on the floor. She began screaming at the top of her lungs about how unfair her mother was. Tricia simply stated, 'Very well, dear, if you won't go to be earlier you will have to miss out on ballet and swimming classes. You need more sleep because you do so many things after school. So you either go to bed earlier or you don't go to ballet and swimming.' Ella pulled herself together almost immediately and began to see some sense in an earlier bedtime.

Emotional blackmail. The purpose of Ella's temper tantrum was to get her own way. She didn't like what she was hearing so she threw a tantrum as a form of emotional blackmail. In this case, her mother remained firm and refused to give in. Magically, the youngster regained control when the display of temper didn't achieve its purpose.

Tantrums are used by kids of all ages as a way of getting something that they want or to demonstrate their disapproval over a changed situation. Older children often sulk, which is a more acceptable form of tantrum.

Tantrums require an audience for them to be effective. In some cases the bigger the audience the better, as they know parents are more likely to give in to avoid embarrassment. Supermarkets, shopping centres, libraries and friends' homes are all excellent places for tantrums. Children sometimes throw tantrums in their bedrooms, but they are always loud enough for someone to hear.

Don't provide an audience. Talking or providing warnings is usually ineffective with young children. When a tantrum begins, move away from the child. Go into another room or even outside. If the tantrum is in public, either move away from your child (still close enough to keep an eye on him) or quietly remove him from the scene. Refuse to be around tantrum throwers. This is an effective consequence related to the misbehaviour.

Don't give in to children's tantrums. Be firm and refuse to be blackmailed. When we give in we're sending a message that tantrums work if children cry loud and long enough. What an effective weapon to have in the armoury!

Get on top of tantrums before they begin. As soon as you see the first sign of a wobbly, act to prevent it. Intervene in whatever way you can to avert them from throwing a tantrum.

Mental water torture whining

'Muuuum, caaan I have a driiink?' Continuous whining is like water torture. It slowly wears us down until we can't stand it any more. As you may have guessed, I have cracked many times under the constant, slow-working pressure that whingeing applies.

Whingeing and whining are particularly effective ways for children to gain a parent's attention or to get what they want. Often kids don't know they're doing it and parents don't realise they're reacting to it. We do it almost instinctively to put a stop to that horrible noise emanating from the mouth of a child.

When faced with whining try the following:

1 Make children aware that they are in fact talking like a wounded animal. A simple reminder such as 'Steve, you know you are whingeing at me' can be enough to put a stop to whining. Often kids are unaware that they're whingeing, especially if they're tired.

2 Put space between you and the whiner. Don't give in to whining requests. Let your child know that although you love him, you don't wish to have the pleasure of his company when he whinges.

3 Make it known that you will only assist children when asked courteously. They will soon get the picture when the salt is passed only when accompanied by a 'please' issued in a reasonable voice.

4 Check the sleep arrangements. Sometimes whingeing kids merely need a rest or a few good nights of sleep.

5 When all else fails, give a chronic whinger a dose of his own medicine: invite him to sit down and hear about your problems. Chances are he'll be off like a shot. He won't put up with a whingeing parent!

Attention-seeking behaviour — what it's all about

Let's get one thing clear. We all like to receive attention. That's not to say that we should receive it all the time. The nature, type and quality of attention given is open to question.

Attention-seeking is the most common form of misbehaviour in children. It is particularly common in young kids as they believe that the world revolves around them. It can take many forms — eating problems, excessive clowning, the walking question mark, excessive cuteness, constant interruptions, thumb-sucking and untidiness. The goal of attention-seekers is to keep parents busy or to put them in their service. Of course, they are usually very effective at gaining attention as such behaviour is difficult to ignore.

But is all misbehaviour for the purpose of gaining attention? No, but misbehaviour by its very nature causes parents and teachers to direct attention to children. To identify attention-seeking behaviour ask yourself, 'Would the behaviour cease if I paid it no heed?' If the answer is yes, then it's attention-seeking, as it requires feedback for it to continue.

Parents feel annoyed by attention-seeking behaviour. 'Stop that, will you, it's driving me crazy' is a typical response. Children who believe that they are significant only when they are noticed or being served are experts at annoying parents. Feelings of annoyance or irritation are a sure guide to identifying attention-seeking activities.

Okay, so they want attention. But why negative attention such as nagging and yelling? In the absence of quality attention, negative attention will do. Children prefer to receive encouragement, know that they are appreciated by others in the family and spend enjoyable time with their parents. When a child doesn't receive enough of the above he or she will settle for negative attention.

What do you do with attention-seekers?

1 Ignore attention-seeking behaviour as much as possible. Impose consequences or corrective procedures in a low-key manner to give them minimum attention.

I witnessed a bored four-year-old who thought he would liven things up a little when his mother had visitors for morning coffee. He began to swing a broom above his head in the living room where the visitors sat. As he was in the midst of the visiting throng, not to mention that he was narrowly missing ornaments with his broom, his behaviour was fairly hard to ignore, to say the least. The boy's mother quietly removed the broom and led him from the room with a minimum of fuss. He received no pay-off for his behaviour and the consequence was that he was no longer welcome in the room.

2 Provide liberal doses of attention on your own terms. You decide when kids receive your attention rather than reacting to misbehaviour. Ensure that children receive good quality attention. This means encouraging them, and

valuing their contribution and personal achievements, as well as spending time with them.

3 Catch children being good. When children are cooperating it's essential to show your appreciation or take an interest in their activity, even for only a short time. Children need to get the message that cooperative behaviour gets more attention than poor behaviour.

4 Spend time with your children. Read, play, chat or just relax together. Enjoy their company. Our limited time with them needs to be enjoyable and fulfilling rather than spent nagging or reacting to poor behaviour.

5 Help attention-seekers feel useful. Then they don't have to resort to cheap tricks to gain a sense of belonging in their own home.

Chapter 6

KEEPING YOUR COOL
IN A CRISIS

'My baby is constantly crying. She is normally a placid child. What do I do?'

'My four-year-old is unhappy at preschool. How do I handle the situation?'

'My seven-year-old's teacher informs me that his behaviour is extremely poor. How can I help him?'

'My teenage daughter came home late from a party last night. I spent most of the night worrying. What can I do with her?'

Raising children has the potential to reduce even the most cool and controlled adult to a bumbling mess. So many of the situations parents deal with are new to them, which is stressful in itself.

There are many pressures affecting parents which would be simpler to categorise as internal (within you) and external (imposed by outside forces). Internal pressures, such as meeting your own needs, feeling frustrated, unfulfilled ambitions and pressure to be an exemplary parent, all add stress to the role of parent. External pressures, such as the demands of children, work, economic necessities, meeting the needs of a spouse or partner, dealing with the pressure of single parenthood and with the expectations of others (such as your parents or friends) can be stressful. And all of these pressures are generally just below the surface.

Do you feel like you're losing control? At times it becomes difficult for us to react to situations as we would like to. Everyone wants to feel that they are always in control, but in reality it isn't always the case. At times we lose our temper or simply don't know what to do. These feelings are natural for many parents who are constantly dealing with new situations and unfamiliar personal territory.

The issue of control is central to raising children. As parents soon discover, it's extremely difficult to control children. They have minds of their own and as they develop they want to exert their independence. The favourite word in a toddler's vocabulary is 'no'. He's letting a parent know that he wishes to do things his way. Older children exert their independence in increasingly sophisticated ways. Even a simple haircut can become a battle of massive proportions as your idea of an appropriate style can vary greatly from your child's.

Stimulation, influence and guidance are far more effective tools than straight-out control. Parents aren't powerless to the whims of their children. Many parents who complain that they have non-compliant children are reactors to children's misbehaviour. By controlling yourself, you can influence kids more than by trying to control or change them.

Jenny constantly nagged her two young children to tidy their toys away when they had finished playing. When she reminded them of their responsibility they would usually blame the other for making the mess and refuse to clean up. When Jenny tried to find out who made the mess they would only argue more. Frustrated by her inability to make them clean up she would send them both to their rooms with a lecture to boot. Her reactions only helped to maintain the misbehaviour.

It would have been far more effective for Jenny if she had focused on factors she was able to control. Jenny could not control her children but she did have other options.

Jenny could have . . .

1 told her children what she was going to do about the mess.

2 confiscated all toys for a period of time until the children had shown a willingness to assume responsibility for them.

3 allocated a play area where the mess would not worry her.

4 altered her routine so that dinner was served when play areas had been tidied.

Jenny was not powerless to the whims of her children. By controlling herself, altering the environment and establishing a routine she could have avoided a situation that placed her in a no-win situation.

Recognise the danger signs of losing your cool

Our body gives off signals when we are losing our cool. Muscle tenseness, inability to relax and a raising of the voice are common external signals. Hyperventilation, blushing and sweating can also be experienced. Internally, the blood pressure generally rises as a reaction to high arousal levels. Learn to recognise these signals so that you can either control your reactions or provide an appropriate outlet for your emotions.

Recognise hot buttons

We all have 'hot buttons' that children can easily press to trigger a reaction. Whining, eating problems, untidiness, swearing and fighting between siblings are common buttons that trigger a strong reaction in one parent yet can be ignored by another. It's important to recognise those behaviours which lead to a strong reaction, as they are the ones which often cause the greatest parental concern.

Watch a young child in a supermarket who wants to provoke a reaction from his mother. He only has to ask for a sweet, stand back and let events run their course. When the request is refused he throws himself on the ground and begins a full-scale tantrum. He knows that this will gain the desired response from his mother, who will either give in and provide him with a sweet for the sake of peace, or provide him with some negative attention in the form of a smack or verbal blast.

Negative attention is far better than no attention, even if it is a little painful. This boy was aware that his mother felt extremely vulnerable to a tantrum in public and he knew the right button to press.

So you've lost your cool, what now?

Will they ever forgive me? The good news is that children are generally extremely resilient and very forgiving. When you have exploded, allow time for everyone to cool down before discussing the conflict. If appropriate, apologise for your actions. This is a sign of strength, not weakness.

Let your kids know that you're human and that, like them, you battle for control at times. I'm not suggesting you throw yourself at their feet and beg forgiveness. Sensibly discuss how their behaviour made you feel (although they will probably have a reasonable idea by now) and perhaps explore ways in which conflict can be resolved.

Children will appreciate this human face, and you will also be showing your children how they can react when they lose their temper and regret their actions.

Stop and think. Train yourself to stop and think about what's happening when children are misbehaving.

Are there reasons for it? By responding respectfully, parents are demonstrating that they are in control of themselves even if they cannot control their children or the circumstances they are in.

Recognise signs of stress in children

Children often let off steam at those who love them the most. A young mother recently described an incident involving her son when she picked him up from school. Jonathon was in second grade. As she was driving home her son began to swear and taunt his younger sister unmercifully. The mother was surprised as this was not his usual pattern. She asked him calmly to stop and explained that it was upsetting her and his sister.

Later, when she was preparing a snack, it occurred to her that something may be bothering her son. 'Jonathon, did anything happen at school today?' He then related his tale of woe. There was a group of boys in his grade who had been teasing him for the last few days and making life a misery for him at school.

The mother, who was very aware of her child's usual behaviour patterns, correctly interpreted that something was amiss with Jonathon when he began to act out of character. She read his pleas for help and understanding and acted in a way that maintained calm and initiated a solution to his problem.

Help kids express themselves. Encourage them to express their feelings in ways that cause the least distress to themselves and others in the family. Help them to recognise and share their doubts, worries, anger, guilt or other feelings. Okay, there may be an initial shouting match or banging of doors, but ultimately feelings are best handled when shared with someone else.

Defuse situations before they escalate

It's far easier to deal with any situation if we are prepared for it. Through thoughtful planning and self-awareness parents can act in ways that reduce unexpected pressure and allow them to remain in control.

'An ounce of prevention . . .'

Consider Antonio, who was working in his study. He overheard the beginnings of an argument between his two daughters over the choice of a TV program. He was faced with the choice of allowing them to settle the dispute themselves or to intervene before World War Three broke out.

Knowing his daughters' propensity for a titanic struggle, and knowing that he had a great deal of work to do in a short time, he chose the latter strategy. He went into the TV room and stated quite firmly that the television would be turned off and the plug removed unless they resolved their dispute quickly.

He offered to sit down and discuss their problem at a later date, however, he was unwilling to do so at this time. When presented with these stark choices the girls reached an agreement almost immediately. They realised that some TV was better than none at all.

Antonio recognised the signs of a potential conflict that would disturb him and acted to nip it in the bud before the situation became too difficult to handle.

There's a time and a place for discipline
The time

When a toddler is thumping the child of a friend who has dropped around for a coffee, discipline needs to be immediate. Either removal from the play area or some time spent in a timeout area may be appropriate.

Not all misbehaviour needs to be dealt with immediately. When adults and children are angry it is more effective to allow those concerned time to cool off and deal with the matter when calmness prevails. Similarly, attempts to discipline children are ineffective when they are over stimulated or excited. There are times when parents need to wait until their youngsters have settled down so that their message can have the desired effect.

The place

It can be extremely difficult to exert your influence over children in public. They often become parent-deaf when surrounded by others or react adversely through embarrassment at being ticked off in front of other people. There may be situations where, as parents, you need to either remove children temporarily from a public situation to provide a warning about misbehaviour, or even wait until you are home to deal with it calmly and rationally.

But I can't ignore it . . .

The majority of children's misbehaviour has the purpose (although not consciously) of gaining parents' attention. If there's no feedback, it tends to stop. When ignoring misbehaviour parents can remove themselves physically or psychologically. If possible, stop what you are doing and move to another part of the house or into the street.

Focus your attention away from the annoying behaviour, either by striking up a conversation with another family member, turning up the radio or TV or becoming engrossed in the activity you were doing.

A mother of three young children recently informed me of her own potent ignoring method. Whenever her children annoyed her with unwarranted demands or aggravating behaviour she listened to music on her Walkman. She claimed that it was the best present she had ever received. She was able to perform her normal duties, free from the whining and squabbling of her children, which she couldn't stand.

Sidestep power struggles

Let's face it, some children just love to challenge parental authority. A simple request is met with a firm 'No, I won't do it'. Many children spend a great deal of energy trying to defeat their parents. Simple commands become invitations to enter a struggle for dominance.

Parents and children agree to fight and argue. It takes two parties to fight in any dispute. Parents can refuse to be drawn into a dispute. It's far more effective to sidestep a struggle and react sensibly to the needs of the situation; for example, when a child refuses to eat he will be hungry. Kids who refuse to pick up toys can have them removed.

Two keys to successful sidestepping

1 Show your unwillingness to be drawn into a fight by letting a child know what you are going to do about a situation.

2 Stop telling children what they should do. By refusing to fight or argue we are taking away the purpose of the behaviour.

By following these steps, we are not giving in to children. We are concentrating control on ourselves rather than pursuing the desire to control our children for the sake of blind authority.

The parent who cries, 'Sophie makes me so mad sometimes', has it all wrong. We are in a position to *choose* how we react to children's behaviour. We can stay and fight or we can refuse to be drawn into a situation of a child's making. When confronted with behaviour that may lead to an angry response, it's better to change activities, leave the room or turn on the stereo in an effort to remain calm and keep control over yourself and the situation at hand.

Power-seekers usually respond when offered realistic choices. The use of choices offers the illusion of personal power as you are effectively placing limits on children's behaviour.

Giving them choices

1 To a noisy child playing inside: 'You may play that game outside or you may choose a quiet game if you wish to remain inside.'

2 To a youngster who refuses to behave at the dinner table: 'You may eat quietly at the table or you may eat your meal in the bedroom.'

Children are less likely to fight with parents when they participate in the decisions that directly affect them.

Time-out

A lot has been written about the use of time-out as a discipline technique for parents. The value of time-out cannot be overstated, however, the way it is used and applied by many parents is open to question. Parents who use time-out as a punishment or deterrent for poor behaviour often become frustrated and claim that 'it just doesn't work with my child'. They are perplexed when they enter their child's room after a ten-minute time-out period to find their youngster happily playing with toys he has discovered. 'Time-out is supposed to unpleasant. He looks too happy for my liking', thinks an exasperated parent.

Time-out is most effective when used to break a child's pattern of behaviour or to interrupt a deteriorating situation. Strictly speaking, time-out is a formal way of ignoring children's misbehaviour. Time-out is a way of removing a child from your attention. This method of training children is excellent for parents who find it difficult to ignore kids when they misbehave or who have a need to be doing something about poor behaviour. Often parents cannot focus their attention away from irritating behaviour. I'm sure many a child's hide has been saved thanks to the break time-out provides.

Time-out is for parents as well as for children. It interrupts a pattern of behaviour and provides parents with the opportunity to change their strategy or the pace of children's activities. It can provide a well-earned temporary respite while you settle your nerves and regain control. It also provides a much needed thinking time when you are stumped as to how you should respond to a situation. Often time-out is sufficient action in itself to bring about a change in behaviour.

Divide and conquer is the principle to be used here. A final word, when providing time-out for two or more children, place them in separate areas of the house or they may continue to misbehave together.

How to use time-out effectively

Parents who use time-out as a form of punishment are generally disappointed. It is more effective when used to break a child's activity, prevent a deterioration in behaviour or provide an over-stimulated child with the opportunity to calm down or regain control.

Time-out allows parents to alter a situation, provide a much needed breathing space or to give attention to other children who are behaving appropriately. It can also be an effective tool if the following points are followed:

1 Time-out areas. Bedrooms make good time-out areas as they are generally private places away from stimulation. However, the use of other more public parts of the house may be appropriate. A minute in the kitchen may be sufficient for a toddler to break his pattern of behaviour and redirect his attention elsewhere.

2 Avoid a punitive attitude. Don't use time-out to teach a child a lesson. It doesn't have to be a nasty experience. Besides, where is the punishment if your child is in his room surrounded by his toys?

3 Adopt a calm, low-key approach to time-out. Rehearse some key phrases to initiate time-out, such as 'Go to your room until you cool down, please.'

4 Time-out doesn't need to be too long. It can last for as little as a minute for toddlers and up to five minutes for older children.

5 The critical phase in the time-out procedure comes at its completion. Parents need to use their energy to redirect a child's attention towards positive behaviour.

Time-out for parents — seven minutes of calm in six steps

When your body is tired, your emotions are screaming out for some relief and your family is demanding that you do six things at once, grant yourself some time-out.

Seven minutes of calm is an unobtrusive way of granting yourself some time-out. It is excellent preventative medicine for tired parents

What you should do

1 Grant yourself permission to stop and do nothing. You have earned a small break. Your children will benefit by having a relaxed parent rather than one falling apart at the seams.

2 Find a quiet place where you won't be disturbed. (Bedrooms are good places to retreat to.) A mother I know has difficulty keeping children from her bedroom so she uses music to effectively block out all noise.

3 Do nothing. Close your eyes and relax. If you have trouble relaxing see pages 24–6 for some ideas.

4 Refuse to become involved in anything that will distract your calm. Blank children from your mind. If you are escaping from some particularly annoying behaviour, don't stew over it or you may over-react when your time is up.

5 Use an egg-timer or alarm if time is short.

6 Resume your normal activities when your time expires.

Why only seven minutes? Don't limit yourself if you can afford more time or need a longer break. Take half an hour if you can. However, many parents don't take a break when they need it most. Claims of 'I just can't afford to stop' are common. Seven minutes is a period of time that causes the least intrusion during a busy day, while still being long enough to gain some tangible relaxation benefits.

Train yourself to take a break whenever you feel you need it.

Chapter 7

MANIC MOMENTS

'**Can't you children see that I'm busy?**' It's five o'clock and Sandra is about to prepare the evening meal. Her six-year-old son Jason nags her to hear him read the book he's brought home from school. Four-year-old Jessica is at her feet reminding her that she's hungry. 'When's tea, mum? I'm starved!' Jessica's twin brother Andrew is playing with some boats in the bathtub and splashing water all over the floor.

Sandra sighs as she starts to tackle another hectic crazy hour before dinner is served. 'Won't you children cooperate with me for a while?'

Identify difficult times of the day

I am convinced that only television families are free of manic times of the day. There would be few parents who can claim that they don't have one hectic time of the day involving their children. For some, getting children up and started is a major effort, while others have no problem at this time of the day, but shudder when bedtime is mentioned. Many cope quite well with bedtime but get in an awful tangle in that crazy hour before dinner when a hundred things need to be done and there is only one able pair of hands.

Mealtime itself can bring nightmares to some parents who find that they are constantly fighting with their children about the amount and type of food they should eat, or their apparent lack of manners and concern for others at the dinner table.

Think of your typical day in terms of blocks of time. For instance, in the morning parents are preoccupied with a vast array of activities to prepare the family for the coming day. Identify the block of time that presents the greatest difficulty (e.g. the morning, after school, or the evening) and structure activities so that noncompliant behaviour is minimised.

Morning madness

Mornings are often chaotic in many households, particularly where both parents work or in the homes of sole parents. Both parents and children have a great deal to do in the morning to prepare for the day. Eating breakfast, making beds, tidying rooms, attending to hygiene, making lunches, cleaning dishes, packing bags and dressing are just some of the morning's activities.

Attention-seekers and dawdlers can find mornings an ideal time to keep parents busy. It is often easier to give in to a child's requests in the morning than to bear the whining and nagging that accompanies a refusal.

Many of the morning difficulties arise due to a lack of clear understanding of the roles to be performed. Perhaps the biggest mistake is the belief that children wouldn't be able to get to school without their parents pushing and nagging them. Most kids, even very young ones, are capable of performing most of the morning tasks without parental interference, yet we so often take these responsibilities away from children.

'**If I fell ill tomorrow, would my children be able to look after themselves in the morning?**' The answer in most cases is an emphatic yes. Children will quite happily allow someone else to take responsibility for their morning activities if they are shielded from the consequences of being late. But mornings, busy as they are, provide the perfect opportunity to develop independence in your kids.

Dealing with morning mayhem

1 **Establish clear routines.** Devise, with your children, an order of events that is understood by everyone. (Make sure you also have a difficult-day routine for children who are overtired or who have woken up in a bad mood.)

2 **Clearly identify tasks.** Identify the jobs to be performed by you and your children. Ensure that everyone in the family is aware of the tasks they are to perform. Kids

should be able to do the routine tasks that directly involve them, such as preparing breakfast, dressing and packing bags and, if they're old enough, making their lunch.

3 **Identify and remove distractions.** Some children become absorbed in television, some spend an eternity choosing their clothes, while others take forever merely locating clean clothes. Be aware of possible distractions and act to eliminate them. Television, if it's to be watched, can be turned on when children are ready for the day. Clothes can be chosen and laid out the night before.

Refuse to be distracted from your own routine by unwarranted fights or arguments that your children may involve you in. When kids miss breakfast due to arguments, they will soon learn to alter their behaviour.

4 **Avoid covering for children's misbehaviour.** Many parents cover for children by driving them to school if they're late or bringing unmade or forgotten lunches to school so that they won't go hungry. Don't. This will ensure that morning madness continues as they know that mum or dad will come to their rescue.

Many parents are unwilling to take such a hard-line approach, but if kids are allowed to experience the consequences of their inappropriate or uncooperative behaviour, they are more likely to behave in the future.

The evening rush hour

The hour before the evening meal is a time when parents, often singlehandedly, are trying to cook while completing tasks such as folding the washing and bathing the kids. It seems that everything needs to be finished by dinner. It's also a time when children's reserves are at their lowest, as they are tired and hungry after a long day.

Nagging, whining and making demands on your time for help with homework are also common at this busy time. The evening rush hour seems to be similar in most families, regardless of the number or age of children, although, in my experience, it is worse when the kids are of a preschool age.

1 **Reduce your activities**. If this time of the day is frantic in your household, consider reducing your routine activities. Parents often try to juggle a large number of activities such as cooking, folding washing, bathing youngsters and hearing children read, aside from responding to undue demands from children.

While some activities are fixed and cannot be completed at any other time of the day, there may be some things that can best wait or be rescheduled. Generally, the less we demand of ourselves during the 'crazy' hour the easier it will be to cope effectively.

2 **Establish activities you can complete.** The evening rush hour is when you need maximum time to yourself, so interaction with your kids needs to be kept to a minimum.

Younger children may need to be kept busy with structured activities that require little adult assistance, such as playing with toys or drawing. Steer away from activities which will excite them or make an excessive mess. Noisy activities are definitely for outside the house. Help young children learn a routine such as play, clean-up, bath and dinner, as this develops their independence and self-reliance. Let older children know that you're temporarily unavailable for meaningful communication or homework. If help is needed then homework is best completed after dinner. Older children need to be involved in undirected activities that require minimum assistance, such as reading or listening to music. If kids need to be driven or picked up from after-school activities, ensure you have enough warning.

3 **Grandma's principle.** It was my grandma who said ice-cream is available only when all greens have been eaten. When a child finds that his dinner has not been served because he neglected to take a bath and feed the family pet (his assigned chore) he is likely to alter his behaviour. This may be accompanied by a temper tantrum, as the child will most likely resent this intrusion as parental interference. However, your actions will have the desired effect if you're persistent.

4 **Withdraw your cooperation when children are uncooperative.** Children need to learn that cooperation is a two-way street. Withdrawing your cooperation means stopping the activity that benefits children, and engaging in a pleasurable one of your own (sitting down, taking it easy) until they begin to cooperate. If they wish to have your cooperation, then they should cooperate.

This often has a magical effect on children, particularly if your interrupted activity was preparing dinner. It also shows that you're serious about your request for assistance at this time of the evening. Children learn extremely quickly when they know that mum or dad is willing to follow their requests with appropriate action.

Mealtimes

The evening meal serves two functions. It is a necessary refuelling time as well as providing an excellent opportunity for conversation. This social aspect is often missing in many mealtimes as the television is blaring in the background or busy children sit down and eat their meals in shifts, or misbehave. Certainly, it can be difficult in many families to have all members present for a single sitting. However, whenever possible, parents should grasp the opportunity to share a meal with their children and catch up on the day's events in a relaxed, friendly atmosphere.

How to survive

1 **Set up a sensible mealtime routine.** A mealtime routine that takes into consideration all of the family's needs will help lighten your load as well as enable kids to plan their activities with mealtime in mind. Involve your children as much as practical in preparing for dinner. They can easily set and place food on the table, remove plates and wash dishes, or pack the dishwasher. Brave parents may even request assistance with preparing and cooking food.

Demonstrate to children that their contribution is not only valued but necessary around this hectic time of the day. Let them know that you are willing to be the chef in your eating establishment but you are unwilling to be part of the waiting or dishwashing staff as well.

2 **Help children establish rules for mealtime behaviour.**
Informal rules such as 'We sit down while we eat' establish useful guidelines for children and teach appropriate behaviours for mealtimes. These informal procedures can be discussed with children at a suitable time (see Family meetings, pages 64–6).

3 **Have simple rituals.** Activities such as washing hands and cleaning messy living areas before dinner signal the start of the eating time. Some families may even share a short prayer or say Grace to signal the beginning of the meal.

Recently, I witnessed an excellent mealtime ritual which helped set a friendly tone for dinner and initiated conversation between family members. At the beginning of the meal, when everyone was settled, the mother asked each of her children, 'What's the best thing that happened to you today?' This prompted an interesting review of the day's proceedings from each child. Conversation grew from this simple question.

4 **Use consequences for fussy eating and misbehaviour.**
It is normal for parents to be concerned about the types and quantities of food that their kids eat at mealtimes. However, it's best not to be overconcerned or children will

learn that you are more worried than they are. This concern can become a potent weapon for attention-seekers and power-hungry kids.

Eating is a child's business and there is little need for parents to interfere in the eating process as long as kids experience the consequences of their decisions. When a child picks at his food and decides not to finish a meal then he is indicating that he's not hungry. That's okay as long as you don't allow him to raid the pantry half an hour later. Instead, he may eat his meal cold or reheat it in the microwave or wait until the next meal, by which time he will be very hungry and will eat the lot.

Children who misbehave or leave the table like jack-in-the-boxes are indicating that they have finished eating. When they have finished dinner, they are demonstrating that they don't want dessert. By using simple, logical consequences, combined with established procedures, parents can minimise many of the misbehaviours that can make mealtime a disaster rather than a pleasure.

Bedtime

'It's time for bed, darling. It's eight o'clock. Come on now, off to bed.'

'Aw, mum! Just five more minutes, p-l-e-a-s-e!'

'No, darling, it's time to go bed. You know that.'

'But mum, this is my favourite show. Can't I just watch a bit more?'

'No, dear. Please go to bed. I've had enough. I've had a long day and I want a bit of peace.'

'Mum, you're mean. All the other kids in my grade stay up until 8.30. Why can't I stay up later too?'

And so the battle continues. This type of exchange is carried out in thousands of homes as kids resist parents' attempts to end the long period of tending children and have some time to themselves. Children are experts at stretching bedtime out through procrastination and persistent cries of 'just five more minutes'. This battle at the end of the day is draining for parents, who are yearning for some time to themselves when they can pursue their own interests, enjoy their partner's company or just put their feet up and relax.

How to get them into bed

A clearly laid-out plan can help alleviate bedtime problems and make this period of the day enjoyable rather than a chore.

1 **Don't get them excited before bedtime.** The period before bed should be a quiet time. Kids can play quiet games, read, watch TV or be involved in a suitably passive activity. If children are to play boisterous games at this time then it's unrealistic to expect them to suddenly switch off when bedtime arrives, especially if they're very young.

2 **Begin a bedtime routine an hour in advance.** Establish a clear routine that signals the end of the day. It surprises me how many parents suddenly spring the news that it's

bedtime on their children. It's little wonder children protest when no warning has been given.

A set routine such as quiet time, drink, toilet and story, lets kids know what is expected of them and enables them to plan their activities accordingly.

3 **Distinguish between being in bed and being in the bedroom.** Children vary in the amount of sleep they need. It's pointless to expect children to be in bed at a certain time each night and then go to sleep. It is realistic, however, to expect children to be in their bedrooms at a set time. They can regulate their own behaviour once they're in their rooms.

After you have said 'good night' in your usual way they may choose to read or play quietly in their rooms, or even in their beds. This should be no great concern to parents as long as children don't interfere in parents' time. Once away from the adult world children generally fall asleep fairly quickly. Younger children may be required to remain in their beds surrounded by favourite toys or a selection of books to keep them occupied until they fall asleep.

4 **Be firm; resist procrastination.** It's important to be firm with procrastinators at this time of night and resist efforts to involve you, such as calls for drinks, last-minute arrangements of teddies and assistance with forgotten homework. Kids soon learn that parents are willing to remain involved with them if enough pressure is brought to bear. Once the kids are in bed ignore them calling out and demonstrate that you are unwilling to participate in

their games. This is your time now and it is extremely precious.

At bedtime begin your usual way of saying good night, whether the kids are in bed yet or not. One parent I know begins by reading a bedtime story. As her daughter treasures her story this is enough to have the youngster rushing to bed every night at the appointed time.

5 **Remove distractions**. Be willing to temporarily remove any distractions from children at this time of the night. In many families this means turning off the TV at bedtime. This often has a dramatic effect on kids as their reason for staying up has been removed. (Of course, when the children are settled you can turn the TV back on!)

6 **Ignore or return boomerangs**. Children who continually reappear after bedtime need to learn that this is not an appropriate time for them to receive attention. Let them know that you're unwilling to provide attention or to become involved in an argument at this time of the day. Ignore them if you are able or, with a minimum of fuss, return them to their rooms. Be persistent and repeat your response if necessary. They'll soon tire of this when they get no feedback

Establishing routines

Flexible routines can be a parent's greatest ally to successfully dealing with manic moments. Routines help children to predict events and provide them with the opportunity to regulate their behaviour. Children generally enjoy a sense of order in their lives. Ask any child what he does at a certain time of the day and he will usually be able to respond with surprising accuracy. Even young kids know what activities usually precede and follow dinner in their household.

Three-year-old Natalia is aware that she takes a bath before dinner and is allowed to have a quiet play immediately after dinner. This order and routine not only provides kids with a sense of security but enables them to learn independence and to assume greater responsibility for their behaviour.

Children differ in their need for structure, even very young children. Some toddlers are extremely adaptable and have the capacity to occupy themselves for long periods of time, whereas others like to have highly planned and detailed activities. It's important to recognise children's individual differences and be willing to be more directive with some children.

Different routines for different days

Everyone has days which are harder than others. Sometimes parents wake up to find that even their easy child is in a terrible mood and is unable to perform his normal morning tasks. It's helpful to have easy- and difficult-day routines for different children, depending on the circumstances.

On difficult days parents can be more directive and provide children with more cues about the types of activities that they can be doing. They should also be more willing and ready to closely supervise children and their activities.

On easy days parents can allow children greater freedom to choose activities (within limits) with fewer reminders and less supervision. Be prepared to alter your routine if necessary. It's important to make a routine work for you rather than be its slave.

You're in control, remember

Many parents waste a great deal of energy trying to badger their children into cooperating during the busy times of the day. They make the mistake of trying to control their children, who have learned at an early age that their parents cannot make them do anything they don't want to do — at least willingly.

Children employ behaviours such as dawdling, temper tantrums, arguing and whining to resist parents' efforts to control them. Don't forget that you have control and influence over the types and sequences of activities that involve you and your child. This is not being manipulative, it's being sensible.

Consider Fatima, who was having a great deal of difficulty getting her kids to school on time each morning. She assessed the situation and realised that her youngsters dawdled not through laziness or a dislike of school, but because they were constantly glued to the TV.

Fatima changed the schedule. She made TV viewing contingent on the kids being ready for school. Only when they were all ready, with all the usual duties performed, was the TV allowed to be turned on.

By controlling the order of activities and making pleasant behaviour dependent on less pleasant activities being performed, parents can avoid unnecessary hassles at the most demanding times of the day.

Changing the scene

Often the change from one time of the day to the next can be difficult for parents. Children often resent and resist what they see as parents' imposition on their time. It may be extremely sensible from an adult perspective that youngsters go to their bedrooms for the night at a certain time, but kids involved in a game or other activity may not see this in exactly the same light. Resistance is common at these times.

It is extremely useful to have established rituals that signal the end of one phase of the day and the beginning of the next. The use of a bedtime story is a time-honoured ritual and extremely useful in signalling that the day has effectively ended for children and that sleep awaits them (see *How to get them into bed*, pages 115–7).

Chapter 8

BUT WON'T YOU CHILDREN HELP!

A family, regardless of its size, should see itself as a team, with members contributing for the good of everyone. The temptation to take on all the tasks to be carried out around the home is very real for many parents. Parents who juggle too many roles (housekeeper, taxi driver, part-time nurse and chef, to name a few) soon find that they start to fall apart at the seams. 'While many of these roles cannot be shared by others, particularly when children are very young, there are several ways in which the heavy load can be shared with other family members.

Children — a help or a hindrance?

Recently, I met a family with eight children, ranging from two to fourteen years. I was intrigued to notice that neither parent looked overly stressed as one would imagine having to care for such a large brood, so I asked about their management strategies. They coped in much the same way as their forebears when families tended to be larger and there were fewer household labour-saving devices.

The load was shared by everyone pitching in to help. These parents viewed their family as eight children capable of helping rather than eight children needing to be helped. A closer scrutiny revealed a simple division of labour. There were tasks that all children were expected to perform, such as making beds, tidying rooms and preparing breakfast, and responsibilities shared between children commensurate with age and ability.

What kept everyone up to scratch? The mother, who was the primary caregiver, was too busy with her own tasks to be concerned about kids who had forgotten to put washing in the dirty washing basket or unpack school bags. Responsibility was given to children at a very early age and they experienced the consequences of forgetting chores.

Kids' help was taken for granted. As the family was well-organised and everyone was aware of what was expected, the kids were prompt to remind each other when jobs such as setting the table were forgotten. The members of this family relied on each other in a very real way for their normal daily existence.

The teamwork principles evolved in this family through sheer necessity can be utilised by families with a more conventional number of children. Meals need to be prepared, houses tidied and pantries filled, regardless of the size of families. Homes can become family-centred rather than revolving around the needs of individual children.

Develop a sense of teamwork

Teamwork doesn't always come naturally to an organisation, whether a family, business outfit or sporting group; it generally requires good leadership and a sense of ownership by all members. When children belong to the family through their own contributions, and also share the problems and difficulties, they begin to believe that this is 'our' family, not just 'mine'. This sense of 'we' rather than 'me' is a powerful motivator for children and parents.

To help or be helped

Many parents have difficulty just getting kids to do chores. They spend so much time nagging their kids to make beds and set the table that in the end it's easier to just do it themselves. This is a common trap that can be alleviated with a little common sense and determination not to give in for the sake of peace.

Chores fall into two categories: personal and family. For example, tasks such as preparing a meal are family ones, as it benefits the whole family, while making beds is a personal task as it benefits individuals.

Divide the tasks. Spend some time listing all the routine chores in your home, ranging from the mundane, such as preparing breakfast, to the more time-consuming, such as driving kids to swimming lessons. The length of this list will surprise you. Divide them into family and personal tasks.

Balance the personal tasks against the family tasks. Carefully examine the list and determine the jobs that you and your partner can do. The remaining chores can be performed by children. This doesn't mean that kids spend most of their free time toiling over a hot stove while you supervise them from behind the pages of your favourite magazine. However, there can be a sensible allocation of chores based upon children's ages, abilities, study requirements and outside interests.

Personal chores equal responsible kids. Encourage kids to take responsibility for their own well-being by putting their clothes in the dirty-washing basket, making beds, tidying bedrooms, packing lunches in schoolbags and putting clean clothes away. Such tasks take up very little time for children but can be extremely time-consuming for busy parents.

Provide choices. Whenever practical, present a list of chores and allow kids to choose, as they're likely to pick jobs which interest them or which they're able to perform. They're also more likely to complete chores if they can choose them.

Rotate unpopular tasks. Naturally, children may need a little persuasion, as no one likes to take on extra work. There will be certain laborious tasks that will be avoided like the plague, so use a roster system. In my family, emptying the dishwasher each morning fits into this category.

Task roster. Consider the use of a roster for some of the more arduous or important tasks. This can be displayed in a prominent place for all to see. Be careful not to have so many items on the roster that it becomes confusing and unworkable. The advantage of a clearly displayed list of tasks is that children can refer to it when needed, and it takes the load off you. For younger children use symbols or pictures instead of words.

Provide reminders. Be willing to remind kids once about chores. It's unlikely that chores are at the forefront of their minds when they're at home. But be careful not to nag or the chore will simply become your responsibility.

Consequences are more effective than constant nagging to teach children responsibility. Serve the dinner even though the table has not been set. You'll find that knives and forks will be fetched in no time as hungry children search out the person who is dragging the chain. Consequences teach children that their contribution is valued and that you are unwilling to do their chores.

Don't overload children. Some parents have reacted too zealously to my spiel on chores during a parenting seminar. With good intentions they have returned home and loaded up their kids with so many chores that the kids become both confused and resentful. Discretion and common sense should be your guide, rather than hard-and-fast rules or procedures.

Set an example of helping for your children. It's easy to underestimate the effect a good example can have on children's behaviour. Demonstrate helping by offering assistance when kids least expect it. Phrases such as 'Can I carry your bag? It looks heavy' show children that assisting each other is a normal part of family life.

Encourage contribution. Positive comments such as 'Thanks for your help with the tidying. It really made my job easier' focus on the contributions kids make to the family. They're more likely to help in future when they know their efforts are valued and appreciated.

Avoid paying children for helping out. Many parents pay their children for helping out at home, which promotes a self-centred attitude to life. A child's early family experiences teach him or her a great deal about how to belong to groups. When we continually pay them to help we teach them to think 'what is in this for me?' rather than 'how can I help out?' In a very practical sense paying children to help out can be very expensive and can mean that we are always putting our hands in our pockets when we want a little help around the house.

Helping is habit-forming

'You're a bit young to do that. When you're older you can try it.' Many parents make the mistake of waiting until children are 'old enough' to be given chores. Unfortunately, there is no definition of 'old enough', so start young! Young children are generally keen to help parents in any way they can, yet are often discouraged. Developmentally, children usually want to help around the age of two or three.

Their enthusiasm can be nurtured by an encouraging attitude and a willingness to break down complex tasks into small skills. Even a toddler can make his bed by arranging his teddies and placing the pillow in the correct place. With maturity he will master the other steps as well.

Parents are often surprised when their requests for help are rejected as children get older. Children rightfully think that parents have done without their help until now and see no reason to change the situation.

Mum and dad, can I help?

Let's look at some areas where children can be of assistance to parents.

Shopping

Shopping with tots doesn't have to be traumatic. Supermarkets are extremely stimulating places full of products and packages of all colours, shapes and sizes. With a little thought and planning, parents can utilise this interesting environment to provide a worthwhile and enjoyable experience. View children as an asset rather than a burden, helpers rather than unwanted company. They are less likely to misbehave and embarrass you if they're kept busy by assisting you with shopping.

'Mum, can we have some Aeroplane jelly?' Use your child's product awareness to your advantage. Even preschool-age children are able to identify the products that you buy regularly. Ask a youngster to identify the biscuits you usually buy and she will have them in the trolley before you can blink.

Turn tasks into fun. Give kids specific tasks. Ask them to find the breakfast cereal, the ice-cream or the

---

Shopping skills

Activities for young kids

- 'John, can you find the big red packet with the yellow stripe?'
- 'Can you see the number 3 on that sign?'
- 'Pass me the smallest jar on the bottom shelf, please, darling.'
- 'Which packet holds the most?'
- 'Please pass me the heaviest jar, Susie.'
- 'Find the letter F on that packet.'

Older children can also be helpful in ways related to their interests, skills and abilities.

Activities for older kids

They can:
- accompany you with a calculator, adding the prices as goods are placed in the shopping trolley,
- be responsible for choosing a certain type of food or grocery item,
- identify 'specials' in catalogues or on displays,
- assist you in writing the shopping list,
- plan a menu or birthday party food list, and purchase the items required.

---

sandwich spread. Kids are generally keen to locate the food they usually eat. You may also encourage them to choose, within limits. For example, 'Can you choose the jam please, Tim? Get either the strawberry or the raspberry jam.' By actively involving children you are keeping them out of mischief, as well as getting your shopping done in half the time.

Supermarkets develop skills. Supermarkets are great places to develop young kids' mathematical and pre-reading skills. With some thoughtful questions and instructions kids can be stimulated in a very useful way.

Household neatness

It can seem that, as a parent, you are always cleaning and tidying the house without seeing any results. You just finish tidying one area and the kids leave a clutter of toys in another part. There is a yawning gap between a child's concept of tidiness and what an adult considers to be neat.

How to help them clean up their act

1 **Establish mess and no-mess areas.** Children's play tends to be messy. Accept this and help them determine the areas where a mess may be made and may remain for a reasonable period of time with minimum hassle to you. A messy area is best located away from 'traffic' and out of sight, if possible. It's also helpful to have no-mess areas where kids are not allowed to play.

2 **Establish simple tidiness rules.** The following hints are examples of useful procedures which set limits and teach children useful tidiness habits:
   • Toys are put away by those who use them.
   • Clean up the old mess before making a new one.
   • Food is to be eaten while sitting down.
   • Clothes are to be left in bedrooms rather than in communal areas.
   • All children's items are to be cleaned away before dinner and prior to bed.

3 **Develop consequences to support the rules and procedures.**
   • When children have the right to play in certain areas then they have the responsibility to clean up after themselves.
   • Toys left lying around can be confiscated for a period of time or placed in a 'deposit box' until such time as the children demonstrate that they are responsible enough to use them.
   • If children are continually messy in a common area then they may temporarily lose the right to use that place.

Consequences teach kids to accept responsibility for their actions.

Bedroom tidiness

The mere mention of bedroom tidiness can cause parents to shrug their shoulders in despair. If you're locked in a battle with a child over the state of her bedroom you are

The deposit box

Parents who have difficulty with kids leaving toys, books, clothing and other personal effects around the house can use 'the deposit box' strategy. It's far more effective than constantly nagging children to put away their possessions.

1 Place a box or basket in an out-of-the-way place in the house, either tucked away, or up high on top of a cupboard. (The laundry or a storeroom are good locations.)

2 Discuss the deposit box prior to its use. Let children know your concerns about neatness, and that the deposit box will be used in preference to nagging. It's action rather than words that will teach responsibility.

3 When kids leave toys, books or other possessions lying around, collect them without saying anything and place them in the deposit box. They can't be touched until the box is emptied.

4 Once a week the children can empty the box and place items in their correct place. Items left in the box can be disposed of in a sensible manner. One mother I know takes the discarded toys to the nearby school to be added to a classroom's play corner. Often kids realise that they don't need certain items any more and are quite happy for them to be given away.

5 Avoid lecturing or scolding the children about leaving items around. Removing items and placing them in the deposit box is a powerful reminder in itself.

in a no-win situation. Children generally see bedrooms as their sanctuaries and strongly resent parental interference. These are places where they can hang posters on walls, display memorabilia and keep junk on the floor.

More often than not families can come to a rational agreement about bedroom tidiness by following a few sensible guidelines.

1 Bedrooms generally are not going to be spotless. Kids live in them.

2 Determine the degree of untidiness that you can tolerate. Mess beyond this agreed-upon point means you are unwilling to enter their rooms to kiss children goodnight or to put clean clothes in drawers.

3 Bedrooms are to be tidied on a weekly basis. This will help prevent an outbreak of typhoid.

4 Untidy rooms have closed doors.

5 Young children need help to make beds, tidy rooms and keep floors clean.

6 Determine the type of assistance you want to give older children. They will then be aware of their responsibilities.

And finally . . .

An integral part of growing up is learning to care for yourself. Parents set the parameters and offer the lead for children to follow. Be persistent with hardened cases who will eventually become more helpful, if only out of sheer necessity, when they realise that you're not going to do everything for them around the home.

Chapter 9

IT'S ONLY SMALL TALK

Talking with our children comes naturally and we don't often give it a great deal of thought. It's something we just do, like preparing breakfast, changing nappies or making school lunches. Why think about it when you can switch over to automatic pilot and still talk to your kids? However, the quality of our communication is vital, as the nature of our talk helps our children to shape attitudes about themselves and form opinions about the world.

Talking and listening help to forge our relationships with children. Through talk we communicate messages, give directions, resolve problems, exchange points of view and gain a window onto another person's thinking.

A lot of our talk with our kids is incidental. We talk to a baby while changing her nappy, converse with a toddler while dressing him and discuss the day's highlights while driving kids home or preparing dinner. This incidental talk is part of life but should not be taken lightly or dismissed as idle chatter. When we communicate with children messages are being exchanged on two levels — the spoken words and the underlying messages, which both help shape children's attitudes to themselves and the world.

There's good talk . . . 'You really know how to cope when you forget your lunch. It was good to see you borrow some lunch from your friends.' When a mother tells her eight-year-old son this, she is conveying an obvious message of approval but the underlying message is also powerful and helps to shape his self-concept. 'Mum thinks I'm pretty self-reliant. Yeah, I suppose I am', thinks the eight-year-old. Children's self-concepts are shaped and influenced by how they think they measure up in the eyes of significant people in their lives, such as their parents.

And then there's . . . A father tells his young daughter, 'You can be so stubborn sometimes. You're very difficult to live with'. This retort, combined with a stern look, sends the message to his daughter that not only is she stubborn but that stubbornness is not a desirable quality to have.

The child can make two things from this. 'Okay, you say I'm stubborn, then I'll be stubborn', or 'Stubbornness is not going to get me anywhere, so I'll lose it'. Both options are undesirable as they give the wrong perspective on wilful behaviour. There are times when sticking up for yourself, also known as assertiveness, is necessary. However, to be assertive all the time is extremely unpleasant for others.

A child's interpretation of events and messages can often be faulty, so we need to be careful about what we say and how we say it. At this point I don't wish to over-complicate matters, but to point out that kids perceive all types of messages, even when we talk to them casually.

Our lives are so busy that a lot of our talk with our partners or children occurs on the run. Today more than ever it's necessary to make time for talk. Set aside some time during the day to communicate with children in a relaxed, enjoyable manner. The value of talk in terms of building relationships with children and enjoyment can't be underestimated. Begin by talking about mundane daily matters and see how easily the important issues emerge. A chat about 'another boring day at school' can lead to a conversation about an array of topics from 'Where do I come from, mum?' to 'Tom's grandfather died last night. Will he go to heaven?' All the terrific stuff that adds spice to the task of raising children.

'My teenage daughter rarely talks to me anymore,' remarked a distraught father. His conversations with his daughter are generally very one-sided and consist mainly of monosyllabic answers, if he's lucky. I asked this concerned parent if he had talked much with his daughter when she was younger. He admitted that he hadn't had a great deal of time for chatting as he was busy with work. He also revealed that even then he did most of the talking and very little listening.

Communication is habit-forming. The pattern for communication was established early and continued as his daughter entered adolescence. Establish clear communication patterns with young children and they are likely to remain for life. Of course, the test comes in adolescence. However, with effort and commitment even teenagers will talk with their parents . . . as long as their friends don't find out.

Good communicators are great listeners

What makes a good communicator? What is their secret? Why is it that some parents can hold terrific conversations with their children about a great range of topics and others have difficulty even extracting the time of day? The magic lies in their attitude. They treat children with respect and view them as social equals, which means they talk to kids as they would talk to anyone else. They believe that children are worth talking to and value the revelations made and information swapped in a two-way conversation.

Good communicators listen more than they talk. They also avoid patronising, lecturing and putting people down. Think of someone who you enjoy talking with or who you go to when things are getting you down. Chances are they value your opinion, are reasonably positive about life, have a sense of humour, are willing to listen and provide a lift rather than criticise you. You generally leave their company feeling refreshed. Like adults, children open up more when people are willing to listen to what they have to say without fear of criticism or ridicule.

Good listeners generally do three things. They make eye contact, listen without making judgments and provide feedback during a conversation. To establish eye contact with someone we generally have to stop what we are doing and give the talker our full attention. With small children it may be necessary to sit down so that eye contact is maintained.

A good listener also provides sympathetic feedback. Kids appreciate it when feedback takes the form of a personal disclosure, especially from parents. Twelve-year-old Sally, who was nervous about going to high school, felt reassured when her mother revealed that she had also been apprehensive about going to school as a teenager. Sally was surprised, as her mother always appeared so self-assured, and also very relieved to know that her mother understood her nervousness.

To listen without judgement is extremely difficult for many parents who wish to offer well-meaning advice. Tom was nine and having difficulty making friends at school. He spoke to his father about his lack of mates. It was really a concern for him as he felt lonely in the schoolyard. His father, who meant well, suggested that he was probably being difficult to get along with. He also said that Tom should look at himself more closely and examine what it was that the other children didn't

like. Tom felt despondent. All he wanted was some understanding; instead he received a load of unsolicited advice
that only made him feel worse. Tom would be less likely
to go to his father the next time he had something to
discuss.

Positive talk
How do you talk to your kids?

* Is your conversation negative or positive?
* Does it consist mainly of put-downs, directions, reminders,
  warnings and threats, or encouragement and discussion?
* Do you feel that you are constantly nagging your kids about
  everything, from their behaviour to forgotten chores?

**Positive or negative talk — which would you and your
kids prefer to hear?** Positive talk is refreshing rather
than draining, as negative talk invariably is. Children are
naturally drawn toward people who speak and act positively. If a lot of your conversation is negative you can do
something about it. With a little effort and concentration
parents can eradicate all negative talk. Impossible, you
say? Try it for short periods of time. Concentrate on one
period of the day until you get it right.

Why not start at breakfast time? When you get the
urge to speak negatively to one of your family, stop yourself, then either say nothing or say something positive.
Try ignoring misbehaviour rather than criticising kids or
reminding them of their duties. They may think that
you've gone off the rails when you fail to respond to them

in your usual way, but they will certainly appreciate the change. When you have breakfast time under control try another time of the day to develop positive talk habits.

Reluctant talkers

Children differ in the way they talk. Some can talk under water while others withhold information as if their lives depended upon it. Most kids fall somewhere in between. Generally, even the toughest nuts will crack and open up, given the right situation and a topic that will interest them. If you have a conversational clam in your family, try some of the following ideas.

Open questions

Often kids don't talk much because we ask the wrong questions or we ask closed questions. Closed questions require a simple 'yes' or 'no' answer. Questions such as 'Did you enjoy school today, Terri?' will generally be met with the standard 'Yeah, it was okay', or 'Nah, it was rotten'.

It's better to use a question which invites a detailed response rather than a monosyllable.

Open questions generally begin with how, what or where.
- 'How does your new teacher differ from your teacher last year?'
- 'What should we do about your pet rabbit when we go on holiday?'
- 'Where would you like to spend next Saturday?'

Questions that require children to express their feelings or ask for opinions usually generate conversation as kids love to have their say on matters which are important to them.

Directed questions

Ask a routine question and you'll get a routine answer unless something really exciting happened and they're bursting to tell you anyway. Ask questions that require specific answers to be given so that kids can't help but open up a little. Questions which direct children to give specific information take a little thought but usually get conversations flowing.

Try asking some of the following questions:
- 'What was the best thing that happened at school today?'
- 'If you could change one thing about school, what would it be?'
- 'What is your favourite time of the day?'
- 'What would you like to do differently in our family?'

As these questions challenge kids to think, it's probably best to ask them when they're relaxed, and not on an empty stomach.

Talk on their turf. Many kids will open up in the privacy of their own bedroom as they feel relaxed and comfortable, but not in public or even in front of others at home, either through fear of embarrassment or shyness. Think of where your child feels most comfortable and least threatened to begin a conversation.

Share a snack and a chat. Some of the most intimate conversations between adults are held when a meal is shared in a comfortable setting. The serving of food has the advantage of anchoring children to one spot at least until it's devoured. Use a snack time or mealtime as an opportunity to start up a conversation about those mundane matters that can so easily lead to fascinating subjects. When kids are given an after-school snack have a coffee break yourself and spend some time with them.

Talk while sharing an activity. When I worked as a teacher, if I wanted to know any gossip about children, I would invariably go to the art teacher, who heard all sorts of fascinating conversations while students were hard at work. It never ceased to amaze me how kids would reveal intimate details while involved in an intricate art activity. They would be relaxed, the hands active and the tongues loose as they spoke about who was going out with whom or what they thought of that new teacher who was giving them a rough time.

Children often divulge personal information freely when sharing an activity with an adult. Boys, in particular, love to do things with their fathers. Much constructive talk between fathers and their sons takes place while dishwashing, gardening, fishing, loading the wheelbarrow with wood or on the way home from a football game. Conversation just flows as closeness is bonded through a shared activity.

In any conversation it's important to respect the other person's boundaries. Be on the alert for any signs of discomfort and be ready to close down the conversation or change the subject.

Establish rituals that promote communication with adolescents.

The best type of communication occurs when adults and children interact quite naturally, through shared activity or playing a game. It is often fun and rarely contrived. Such communication is relatively easy to engage in with pre-school or primary school aged children as they generally want to be around their parents. However parents need to be a little more pro-active to create opportunities to communicate with adolescents who increasingly lead separate lives to their parents. The establishment of a number of social rituals involving adolescents and parents provides opportunities for you to stay in touch with young people and promote healthy relationships.

Two rituals that bind.

1 Once every two or three months have a regular meal or outing with each adolescent in your family—but keep it one-on-one. Take your time, have a chat but don't get heavy with deep and meaningful conversations. Schedule it in your diary and insist that they do the same. Kids need to learn that there are certain activities that are non-negotiable and regular time with a parent is one of those.

2 Have open mealtime once a month where your teenage

children can invite their friends around for a sit-down meal. Experience in my own family has shown that this is a great way to meet their friends and find out what is happening in their lives. As a wise parent, just serve the meal, join them and don't interrupt. I have found out more about what is happening in my children's lives at these mealtimes than at any other time.

Encouraging talk

Have you ever wanted the floor to open up and swallow you? I had such an experience some time ago when I was giving a talk in front of seventy people. My nerves got the better of me and my mind just would not function the way I wanted it to. My well-prepared lecture disintegrated as I prattled on. I left the stage in a daze whispering, 'Never again!'

My supervising lecturer (I was a student at the time delivering my first talk on raising children) noted, 'You managed to create a really good rapport with the audience'. This was true. I made a mess of the topic but the audience did respond to me, despite my nerves.

'Now let's look at how you can improve for next time.' I was persuaded back on the stage largely due to my lecturer's encouragement. She could have criticised me for any number of errors that I made, instead she focused on the one positive result — my ability to relate to the audience. That was real encouragement.

Encouraging talk is a skill we can learn. It's useful not only when dealing with kids but with everyone.

The language of encouragement

- focuses on strengths; for example, 'You're really good at . . .'
- recognises improvement and effort; for example, 'You have really improved in . . .'
- shows confidence in the ability of others; for example, 'I know you can do it'
- focuses on contributions made; for example, 'I really appreciate the . . .'

Encouragement helps children develop a positive view of themselves. Sometimes we need a little prompting to remind us to speak positively to children. Often it's helpful to link encouragement with another activity. Get into the habit of offering an encouraging remark when you say goodbye to kids in the morning, greet them after school, and when you say goodnight.

At least you will have encouraged your children three times a day. That's good stuff. Come on, you can do it.

Setting an example

Every move you make . . . A series of anti-alcohol advertisements screened some years back on Australian television portrayed two school kids playing 'mothers and fathers'. The young girl, adopting a traditional house-wife's role, asked her 'husband' to run down to the shops to pick up a forgotten grocery item. The young 'father', lounging back in his chair, replied that he would do the errand as soon as he finished his beer. It's not difficult to work out where both children had learned to act in such ways. The ad concluded with the words: 'Every step you take, someone is watching'; in this case it was two rag dolls in the corner. A chilling reminder for parents.

Parents need to be aware of not only what, but how they say something. A mother complained that her children often shouted at her and insulted her. While discussing the apparent cause of their rude language it was obvious that she spoke to them in a similar manner. She referred to her kids as 'little cows' and frequently worse, and admitted that she often gave them 'a good serve if they deserved it'. As their primary role and speech model, it's no surprise that she received a 'good serve' in return.

Parents are virtually the only language models for preschoolers. They are exposed to different types of speech through the TV and other family members, but the parental influence cannot be overstated. I was once stunned to hear my then four-year-old daughter say to a friend during a dress-up game, 'Come here, darling. Now listen to me.' It was as if I were listening to a tape recording of myself. It sounded so awful I decided then and there to never say it again.

Speak to children as you want them to speak to you. This maxim is true for kids of any age. If we want them to support and encourage others then they must be exposed to positive and encouraging language. And they need to hear it often. Children who are brought up on a diet of encouragement are more likely to encourage themselves and speak positively to other children and adults.

Seven deadly sins to avoid when talking with kids

1 **Lecturing.** 'When I was a boy we didn't have many toys and we looked after everything we owned. Nowadays, you children have so many toys that you just don't value them like you should. You really should . . .' No one likes being lectured. We tune out rather than listen to the lesson that is being given.

2 **Put-downs and criticisms.** 'You're a silly boy. You always forget to give me the school notices. You are so unreliable.' Tell a child often enough that he is stupid and he will soon believe it.

3 **Talking down to/patronising.** 'Oh, you poor thing. That boy was mean. There, there. You can't help it if others pick on you, can you?' Talk to kids honestly and openly rather than in a condescending manner, and they will respond in kind.

4 **All talk, no listening.** Whoever is responsible for the maxim 'Children should be seen but not heard' has a lot to answer for. Question, reflect, provide feedback and give your point of view, but don't dominate conversations to the point that kids can hardly get a word in. Listen, listen, and then listen some more. Listening is the hardest part of communicating!

5 **Labelling children, not the behaviour.** 'What a naughty boy you are!' 'You're a real little liar.' 'You're such a shy child.' In each case a label has been placed on a child, like a badge. It's the behaviour that's
continued

inappropriate, not the child. Separate the behaviour from the person and you're giving them the chance to change their way of acting.

6 **Shouting.** For some reason many adults believe that the louder they talk the more chance they have of being heard. Shouting merely produces 'parent-deaf' children. Shouting may be high on impact but it's very low on effectiveness.

7 **Blockers.** 'What mess did you get into this time?' 'You should have known better than to . . .' 'I knew that would happen.' It only takes one negative comment to silence kids. It's easier and more effective to open up communications by exploring solutions, listening, and empathising with a child.

Encourage open communication

Some families can discuss anything. No subject is taboo in some households, whereas others like to set limits on what is discussed in a family setting, as some subjects can be a little touchy, to say the least. Well-adjusted families are able to talk about most things.

Kids should be encouraged to come to parents with their problems, talk about ideas and topics that interest them and resolve conflict through discussion. Healthy, functioning families operate in a climate of open communication, where mutual respect is practised and individual dignity maintained. It's also essential to keep the lines of communication open as kids grow to be teenagers.

Develop an atmosphere in which opposing views are accepted and display a willingness to discuss the thorny questions teenagers want to ask without imposing your views. This doesn't mean you become a doormat who will accept anything teenagers have to say. Be honest and challenge their views but be willing to accept that they may have excellent grounds for beliefs and values that may differ from yours.

An openly communicating family is one in which:

1 Children's opinions are valued, even if they differ from those of their parents, as different opinions are a sign of independence. Different opinions should be discussed and challenged for validity rather than squashed or ignored.

2 Regular discussions are held about a range of topics, from sport to environmental issues to personal matters. Children are encouraged to talk to each other and their parents without fear of ridicule or put-downs.

3 Emotions are discussed, not avoided. Recognise when your children are sad, angry, happy, frustrated or whatever and help them verbalise and share their feelings. Dealing with children on an emotional level can be hard for parents. We so often glibly say, 'You'll feel better after a good night's sleep'. It's not always the case. A problem can still be there in the morning and emotions still need to be dealt with.

4 A high level of trust and confidentiality is maintained.

Chapter 10

BEING FRIENDS WITH YOUR CHILDREN

It's natural to want to be a friend *and* parent to your kids. Friends talk to each other, enjoy each other's company, have fun together and develop special relationships. At times, however, it's difficult to be both to your children. Parents have the task of teaching youngsters about appropriate behaviour, nurturing their development and teaching them a variety of physical and social skills. They also assume an advisory role when their kids encounter difficulties and problems at school, either with their teachers or peers, or as adolescence approaches.

Remember the days when children were expected to 'respect their elders' and 'be seen but not heard'? Adult–child relationships have changed over the last few decades. Kids are now encouraged through schooling to develop an independent voice, express opinions and challenge ideas. While this may be seen by many people as a disturbing development, it does reflect a trend in the wider society to question the existing role of authority, and relationships based on inequality. Kids, too, are no longer willing to accept an inferior status.

So what approach do I take with my children? Mutual respect and equality are the two values fundamental to all meaningful friendships. Mutual respect implies that parents and children respect each other's rights and dignity while maintaining self-respect. Mutual respect is developed through the use of firmness and kindness: kindness expresses respect for children, their dignity and their views, while firmness gains their respect.

Don't be a doormat. To gain respect from kids it's essential that parents respect themselves and refuse to be walked on by their kids to get their own way.

Social equality means that within limits children can determine their own behaviours. This doesn't mean they can do anything they like. This is anarchy and totally inappropriate as kids must learn to live within the rules and boundaries of different social situations. However, when children are able to determine their behaviour and experience the consequences of their choice they develop self-discipline and responsibility even from an early age.

Guidance, stimulation and influence, rather than direct control, are appropriate strategies to use with children. Friendship is communicated when we treat children with respect and allow them to maintain their dignity even when being disciplined.

'**I love you heaps.**' It's great to hear this and it makes you feel good when you say it. Children need to hear it often. It goes without saying that parents love their kids. We express it in our actions but we also need to express it in words. Babies, toddlers, primary school children and adolescents should be told that they're loved frequently. I have seen many fathers who feel extremely awkward saying 'I love you' to their sons, particularly to teenagers. There is still a belief that 'real men' don't say 'I love you' to each other. When we tell our children we love them they may even return the favour!

Sharing time and activities with children

When I was teaching a few years ago, I had a chat to a group of nine-year-olds in my class just before Christmas. I asked the inevitable question, 'What do you want for Christmas?' Most of them gave me a long list of the latest toys and games.

One young boy gave a different answer that obviously came straight from the heart. 'I don't really care what I get. I'm sure I'll get something good. What I want is my dad to play with me on Christmas morning.' He just wanted his father to spend some time with him. He wasn't worried about expensive gifts or gadgets that are capable of doing everything except his homework. He wanted something more precious than this — some of his father's time.

Time spent with children is rarely wasted. It's like money in the bank, a good investment for the future. Interest is paid in terms of establishing a strong rapport with your youngsters. Time spent in the company of children pays dividends when we learn about their interests and hobbies and, more importantly, the way they think. It also gives us the opportunity to influence their thinking and help develop interests that may remain with them for life.

When my son was young, I went for a walk with him in the bush near our home. I was stunned by his knowledge of the different types of birds we saw. I was surprised that he could not only name most of the birds we came across but had a good knowledge of their habits and habitats. I extended this knowledge by purchasing a number of books about birds and helping to choose appropriate books when we visited the library. This was a worthwhile interest that I cultivated. My son and I had a common interest that continued as he grew older.

Having fun together

Theories abound about how best to promote relationships between parents and children. However, it's easy to overlook a simple, cheap way of forming family friendships — having fun together. When people share enjoyable experiences together, not only do they get to know each other better but they form a bond. Besides, it's harder to fight and argue with someone when you enjoy their company.

The range of fun activities is endless. They do not have to be expensive or require extensive planning. A vigorous game in the park, a picnic or a game of cards are simple, enjoyable activities that can be shared by parents and children.

Children of all ages are experts at playing. They really know how to have fun and enjoy themselves. It's refreshing to enter the world of play that they create. It's also a great way to relax and forget about your worries, if only for a short time. Games can be as simple as a wrestle on the floor or a romp around the backyard, or as complex as matching wits with an older child over a boardgame. The range of games is endless. Choose games that both you and your children enjoy so you can both have fun.

Kids of all ages love to play games with their parents, even teenagers. The trick is to choose games that not only interest them but provide them with a chance of winning. Adolescents generally love to clean their parents up, regardless of the field of battle. If you haven't played any games lately and you're stuck for ideas, consult with them or gain some inspiration from the following activities.

Let them see your game-playing side. In two-parent families ensure that both parents share the fun. In many families one adult takes on the role of playmaker while the other parent is responsible for tasks such as cooking and washing. This is not always a conscious decision, but rather the roles that parents choose generally evolve over time. Children benefit from seeing both

Playing games

- **Vigorous games.** Girls and boys of all ages enjoy playing games such as tag or keepings off, where they have the opportunity to let off some steam.

- **Ball games.** Almost any shaped or sized ball can be used. Informal games such as catch and poison ball are great for people of all ages.

- **Imaginative activities.** Young children love to play dress-up, hold parties and role play adult activities. Kids love to see adults involved in these activities, if only for a short time.

- **Indoor games.** There is a host of boardgames available which are suitable for the entire family. These range from educational-type games to activities that are purely for fun. The humble deck of cards can be put to great use with children.

- **Group games.** It's a good idea to have a store of activities and games that the whole family can play. There are several games available although it's not necessary to buy expensive, complicated games to have fun. My family has a great deal of fun with the simple Snakes and Ladders boardgame.

- **Activities just for two.** Try to have a store of activities or games that you can play with individual kids. A little one-to-one play is a great way to establish a bond with a child.

sides of parents, and when we play with them we relax and reveal a lighter side that they may not otherwise see. Since we strengthen our relationships with our children when we play together, it's only fair that both parents share in the fun.

Some final words about games. It may be necessary to teach kids some of the social game-playing skills, particularly if you play competitive or 'winning' games. Many children, young and old, play games to win rather than to have fun. Continue to emphasise the role of enjoyment and help them to deal with their inevitable defeats. Ignore the tantrums that sometimes occur when things don't go their way. Be firm and refuse to let poor losers or painful winners spoil the fun. They will gradually come around.

Show your children the real you

Many children have an unrealistic view of their parents. They have this notion that you have been an adult forever, and even if you were a child you breezed through that period with little difficulty. You may lose your temper now and then but generally you are in control. While I'm not suggesting that we burden children with our worries it is appropriate to let them know that as human beings we may have doubts, anxieties and frailties that we deal with regularly. Through conversation we can open for our children a window to our thinking and our feelings. They like to know what makes us tick, just as we would like to get inside their heads for a while.

My two youngest daughters used to quiz their grand-mother exhaustively about me as a youngster. They still delight in informing me of misdemeanours, embarrassing moments and incidents that I had long forgotten. They are forming a picture of me that somehow helps to complete their own puzzle of who they are and where they came from. Hopefully, the picture they are forming is a positive one.

Read with children

Books are for sharing. Reading is a cheap, enjoyable, educational activity that can be done with kids of all ages. Parents are generally diligent about reading to pre-school children and kids in the early years of school. However, when children become independent readers we often forget that they enjoy hearing stories. Vary their literary diet by choosing picture storybooks, poetry and novels appropriate to their levels and interests.

Children at the upper end of primary school still

TV-free day

Television is a powerful attraction for most children. It has the ability to maintain their interest while requiring them to exert minimum mental and physical effort. Children's use of TV is a concern to many parents and educators. It is a much overused medium that keeps kids from chores, homework, physical activity and the opportunity to entertain themselves. It invites kids to be passive watchers rather than active participants. TV, by itself, does little to

continued

promote interaction or conversation unless it is used as a basis for discussion. Neither does it require watchers to use their imaginations as they do when they read books.

TV does have its good points. It's a valid form of relaxation, particularly for kids after an arduous day at school. Many programs are high quality in terms of educational content. They expose children to a range of issues and ideas that can stimulate their interest in a way that books cannot. Science and nature documentaries are generally extremely informative for young watchers. However, there are at least an equal number of programs that can be best described as time-fillers, offering little in terms of informative or entertainment content.

Control that TV set. It's essential to control TV viewing and not to allow the TV to be the master of your family. The usual position of the power switch should be the 'off' one. It needs only be turned on when there is something to be watched.

If you decide to be the master of your TV, take the next step and institute a TV-free day in your home. Once you have announced this to your family and the howls have died down, explore alternative forms of entertainment. Join kids in playing board or card games, listen or play music, share a book, or even swap stories and tales about a variety of topics. Make the night so good that the kids look forward to it. It may even be known as the games day rather than 'the day when our parents won't let us watch the telly'.

generally enjoy reading picture storybooks with adults, particularly if the illustrations are stimulating and the characters are easily identifiable. Visit the library with your kids and let them choose books they would like you to read with them. Don't be dismayed if what they choose is of questionable literary or educational value. Most adults like to read light material some of the time too.

When reading with children the emphasis needs to be on enjoyment. This not only promotes a love of books and reading but it ensures that the activity is rewarding for everyone involved.

Chapter 11

WHAT ABOUT SOLE PARENTING?

The number of sole parent families has increased dramatically over the last two decades. Although the sole parent profiles are varied, the difficulties faced are similar. Parenting is a difficult task and certainly much harder than many sections in society give it credit for. The parental workload is doubled for sole parents, as only one parent is available to carry out the tasks of raising and nurturing children.

The profile of single parents is extremely varied

- Separation and divorce rates have increased and more people have made the conscious decision to raise children on their own.

- Although the majority of single parents are women, the

number of fathers who are raising children on their own has also increased in the last decade.

- Single parents who are women are more likely to raise children full-time, although the number of single mothers who work is increasing.

- Single mothers are more likely to work in paid employment if they worked before a separation.

- More single fathers hold jobs than stay at home. This is largely dependent on the age of the children. Where children are of school age, fathers tend to enter the workforce.

The common factor linking sole parent families is financial restriction. Whether a person is fully employed or a full-time parent, financial pressures are always present. Working parents tend to use a significant proportion of their income on childcare, while parents dependent on welfare payments or child support are always trying to make ends meet. However, finding a job doesn't necessarily mean financial independence. Money can remain a dilemma for parents even if they enter the workforce, as payments from other sources decrease proportionately to the income they receive.

Personal difficulties
Personal needs
'**I could use a break.**' Single parents have great difficulty satisfying their own personal needs, whether it be

maintaining adult friendships or relationships, exercise or relaxation. The balancing act that all parents face between caring for others and caring for themselves is even more precarious when there is no partner to offer support, share the load or provide time away from the family. It's little wonder that many single parents complain that they always feel tired or mentally stale.

Children can easily become the focus for single parents. This is often more evident in the early days following a separation, when children fill a void left by the partner's departure. Due to feelings of guilt or concern for their children's welfare, many parents overcompensate and place their kids before themselves. Social invitations and offers of assistance are refused and participation in community events decreases. This is a natural reaction but should not become permanent, as sole parents soon find themselves isolated in a diminishing social circle, and then find it increasingly difficult to say 'no' to their children's requests.

Helena's children had a far better social life than she did. Helena, who is the mother of three children aged twelve, ten and seven, recently separated from her husband. Initially, she threw herself into raising her kids, determined that her children were not going to miss out on anything as a result of her marriage breakdown. Helena gave up most of her outside interests because she was too busy driving her kids to sport, music practice or to friends' houses.

As Helena wanted to look as though she was coping,

she turned down offers of assistance made by family and friends. These offers soon dried up, along with social invitations. In only a few months, Helena had not only lost her partner but her social life. She found herself isolated and in need of a great deal of support. Helena had neglected to maintain a balance between her personal needs, which were obviously great at the time, and those of her children.

Helena made some significant changes to her lifestyle, starting with her refusal to be her kids' full-time taxi-driver. She explained to them that she needed her own time, and took up her relatives' previous offers to babysit so that she could pursue personal interests. Helena made it known to her friends that she was back in circulation by inviting them over for coffee, dinner or even a game of cards.

As most of her friends were married, she had a need to seek out women in similar circumstances to her for feedback and support. By joining a Parents Without Partners group, Helena was able to broaden her network to include sole parents. She was careful though to keep a balance between the types of people she mixed with. Although Helena still found the job of sole parenting extremely difficult, she realised that her coping skills had improved since she had made time for herself.

What about the children?

Sole parents often spend a great deal of time worrying about the fact that children don't live with two parents.

They're naturally concerned about the effect a separation may have. However, sometimes this concern is needless, as kids are extremely resilient and adaptable. I'm constantly amazed at how they can adapt to change, and their ability to live in extremely testing circumstances. **Was it because I didn't put my toys away?** If two partners have separated, it is important to explain to children that they're not to blame. They can often have feelings of self-recrimination and believe that somehow their behaviour led to the separation. Assure them that the split occurred due to a breakdown in the marital (and not parental) relationship. While the children will feel the effects of that breakdown, they will know they did not cause it. Help them to understand that although you and your partner, as a couple, had, and still may have difficulties, as individuals you are no different.

Mum, when's dad coming home? After a separation, much discussion is needed to help children work through their emotions and deal with the difficulties they may encounter. Some children have difficulty accepting the fact that the family unit as they know it has changed. They may have hopes for a reconciliation. It's essential that children face the reality of the situation as soon as possible. The quicker they come to terms with a separation, the sooner they will adapt to the inevitable changes. Focus your children on the future rather than leaving them hoping for a return to the past.

The notion of sharing the parenting following separation may sound like a contradiction in terms but many couples successfully combine their efforts to raise children even though they are separated. It may sound trite but it is essential to differentiate your children from your spouse following a separation if both sides are to act in the best interests of children. This requires separated couples to put their personal animosity aside and take a shared approach to child-rearing including: discussing children's problems, sharing educational decisions, both parents attending parent-teacher interviews and generally both contributing to children's well-being.

Increasingly in Australia we are seeing shared custody of children following divorce or separation with many children spending equal amounts of time with each parent. These shared arrangements mean that both parents can maintain their relationship with their children and avoid the exhausted parent syndrome that is so common amongst sole parents. Equal custody also gives children access to two gender models, which is important for both girls and boys. There is a large body of research to show that the best outcomes for kids following divorce occur when couples maintain amicable relations particularly where access is concerned and when the level of income that existed before the breakdown is maintained. Let's hope the trend towards shared custody continues to increase.

Am I doing a good job?

Understandably, many sole parents feel insecure about the way they raise children. They are responsible for all the discipline (which may have been a task left to the other parent), decision-making, and resolution of problems which may arise. Problems at school, behavioural blow-outs and sibling fighting are also harder to deal with when there is no one to discuss approaches with.

It's natural to think, 'Did I do the right thing? Have I made the correct decision? Am I being unfair or too tough?' It's important to receive feedback about parenting so that we know if we are making the right decisions and adapting a balanced approach between what is right for your child and meeting the needs of the situation.

Share the load. If you have an amicable relationship with your ex-partner then share the load within the established limits. If no such relationship exists, then it's essential to seek advice or someone to discuss issues with elsewhere. Discuss parenting matters with friends, family or agencies which offer assistance (see pages 169–70). It's important not only to seek out ideas but to gain reassurance and support from other people.

'If I had stayed with my husband my son wouldn't have gone off the rails.' Some single parents look to themselves when behavioural problems arise. They sometimes blame the marriage breakdown or their children's lack of contact with two parents for any poor behaviour that kids may exhibit. But such self-castigation is pointless and harmful to your relationship with your kids. It also fails to take into account one important factor about human beings: we're all able to choose the way we behave. No one or no set of circumstances makes us behave in a certain way.

'Look, no wonder he's so rude. He comes from a single parent family.' Too often people look for excuses when children behave poorly. This is absurd thinking, totally unfair on parents and denies the fact that children are capable of making their own decisions about how they behave, regardless of their upbringing. Sometimes the circumstances children are raised in are less than ideal, but that doesn't mean they should be excused if they behave badly. Kids are more adaptable than you think and are able to function well in very difficult circumstances.

Getting the help you need

'The children are so demanding and take up so much of my time that I never have any time for myself.'

'Sometimes I'd like to talk about the kids with someone.'

'I worry that my sons don't see me relating to anyone else. They must have a very one-sided view of adult relationships.'

'As a sole father it concerns me that my two daughters don't have a woman to talk to. I try my best, but there are some things that only a woman can handle.'

'It's frustrating not being able to spend time with my children individually. I just can't share myself around.'

These statements reflect some of the difficulties parents face raising kids on their own. In the absence of a partner to ease the load and share the problems with, it's essential to establish a reliable support network. Family, friends and support agencies can be used by sole parents to provide some time off, physical assistance or merely to maintain sanity.

Grandparents

Grandparents, if available, can be a tremendous asset for sole parents. They can often fill the void created by the absence of a role model or parent of the same sex as their grandchildren. They also tend to be less embroiled in the emotional wrangle created by a separation. It's a tragedy that children's grandparents on their non-custodial parent's side frequently have diminished contact with their grandchildren. Grandparents are often the innocent victims of a separation.

Sole mates

Some parents are fortunate as they have an abundant source of relatives and friends who can support them. Where help is not readily available, it may be necessary to actively seek out a group of people in the same position who can share the load and at least provide you with some time away. There are number of associations or agencies that can be used to provide support for sole parents. In Australia there are Parents Without Partners groups in all states which provide tremendous support such as welfare assistance, emergency accommodation and social activities.

Local government

Local governments are a good starting point for people who are having financial hardships, discipline problems with children or if they are isolated. Community Service departments in each state can provide a list of agencies and organisations that can provide the type of support needed. Often help can be very close to home when we are willing to ask for it.

Parents Without Partners

Victoria

(postal address)

PO Box 21 Canterbury VIC 3126

or

220 Canterbury Road

Canterbury VIC 3126

Tel: (03) 9836 3211

New South Wales

(postal address)

PO Box 388 Wentworthville NSW 2145

or

75 Wentworth Avenue

Wentworthville NSW 2145

Tel: (02) 9896 1888

South Australia

186 Hampstead Road

Clearview SA 5085

Tel: (08) 8359 1552

Australian Capital Territory

(postal address)

PO Box 465

Dickson NSW 2602

or

65 Hawden Street

Dickson ACT 2602

Tel: (02) 6248 6333

Queensland
126b Golda Avenue
Salisbury QLD 4107
Tel: (07) 3275 3290

Tasmania
25 Spring Street
Claremont TAS 7011
Tel: (03) 6243 5007

Western Australia
Oasis House
37 Hampden Road
Nedlands WA 6009
Tel: (08) 9389 8350

Northern Territory
PO Box 4290
Darwin NT 5794

Solace

Solace is a support group for widows and widowers.

Victoria
Tel: (03) 9384 1722

South Australia
Tel: (08) 8272 4334

New South Wales
Tel: (02) 9519 2820

Western Australia
Tel: (08) 9245 4645

Parents Without Rights

This organisation is based in Victoria and provides advice and support for sole parents with custody or access problems. Contact address is PO Box 130, Glen Iris, VIC 3146.

There are various organisations which exist in each state that offer help for sole parents. Check in the Community Services section of your local telephone book.

Be organised

Sole parents need to be well organised. Structure and

a well-established routine are paramount if sole parents are to attend to domestic duties, spend time with children and still have time for themselves. An established routine helps kids to coordinate their activities as they know clearly what is expected of them and can plan accordingly.

Often children of single parents are given a great deal of responsibility, particularly if the parent works. Children generally respond well when given greater control over their own well-being. They frequently develop independence at an earlier age than many kids in dual parent families. Let's look at how two parents used their organisational skills to promote responsibility in children and provide some well-earned time for themselves.

Melanie and Simon: two case studies

Melanie has raised two children on her own for three years. Although only four and six years of age, both of her kids prepare their own breakfast each morning, dress themselves and generally fend for themselves with limited supervision. Melanie ensures that all domestic duties are performed while the children are at preschool and school. She also finds time to exercise daily and take in a craft class once a week.

When the children arrive home Melanie devotes the pre-dinner time to them. She views this as children's time, even though they may have friends around. Dinner is a shared experience held at the same time each night.

continued

After the kids are in bed, this is Melanie's time, to do as she wants. She has one rule which she lives by to keep her sanity — to do one thing for herself every day. Melanie believes that she is just as important as her children so she allows herself to come first at least once a day.

Simon, who recently separated from his wife, has three school-aged children. He works in a professional position near his home. At first he found he was unable to cope with the tasks he had formerly shared with his wife. Morning was the hardest, as he had difficulty organising himself, let alone his kids. To relieve the pressure on him, Simon decided to leave the kids to their own devices. They prepared their own breakfasts and lunches (which received howls of protest at first).

Simon was unconcerned with the state of their bedrooms, as he just couldn't afford the time to nag his children about bedmaking and bedroom tidiness. The bedrooms were invariably untidy but he learned to ignore the mess. With the aid of his kids, Simon established a roster of chores which included preparing meals, washing and ironing clothes, and some house cleaning. He was concerned at first that it was unfair placing so much responsibility on his youngsters, but he had little alternative as he was unable to afford paid home help and found he was falling apart at the seams trying to combine domestic duties with work.

Simon's children responded favourably to the new structure and he was pleased to see that his family worked well as a team. There were times when jobs were forgotten but everyone pitched in and helped as the kids were aware that if they didn't pull together they wouldn't survive as a family unit.

Dealing with the guilts

Sole parents can feel guilty about many issues. Just look at this selection:

- 'I can't provide for them as I would like.'

- 'My kids lack a woman to relate to.'

- 'I should be with my child but I must work to support him.'

- 'I want some time to myself but I just can't leave my baby with someone else.'

- 'If only we hadn't split up then my son wouldn't have gone off the rails. It's all my fault.'

- 'I'd love to spend some time with each of my kids. I wish there were two of me.'

- 'Felicity deserves two parents. She's a good kid and she worries about me.'

This kind of guilt is a form of mental anguish we put ourselves through when circumstances are beyond our control. It's an excuse for being miserable. Guilt left unchecked can be the catalyst for many problems such as alcoholism, drug dependence and physical abuse. It's a highly destructive emotion.

The good news is that guilt can be dealt with and pushed away. So take control, determine that you won't repeat any past mistakes and look at the positive side. Feel pleased with your efforts at raising your children on your own. After all you're doing one of the toughest jobs single-handedly.

Children are extremely resilient. You may think that they are missing out because they're being raised by one parent. But the important aspects of raising kids, such as providing love, care and a stable home life, can be given by one parent. Children and young people gain a sense of protection and security from the existence of a close relationship with at least one person who is capable of expressing affection and who is consistently available to them.

PS Sole parents need time off too. Don't feel guilty about having some time for yourself where you can pursue your own interests. You will be a better parent because of the break.

Self-confidence

'If only I were a better parent, she wouldn't act so stupidly.' A lack of self-confidence can often occur after a parental separation. This decrease in self-esteem can affect the way we as parents relate to children and how we deal with routine discipline issues. Frequently, when our confidence is lacking we blame ourselves for children's misbehaviour. It's easy to lose perspective about inappropriate behaviour and begin to generalise about kids. A child who is caught telling a fib can suddenly be seen as a liar of grand proportions as we overdramatise the situation. 'You're always telling lies', claims a distraught parent. **Poor self-esteem is a result of the isolation that many sole parents feel.** It's important that sole parents remain in touch with the community. Robyn, a single mother of two young children, related the difficulties she had in socialising with other parents in her school community. She found it difficult to attend school functions at night or join any of the parent committees as she had no partner to mind her kids. She felt that she was cut off from mainstream events. Robyn didn't have any family living nearby who could babysit, and she couldn't afford to pay a babysitter.

As Robyn didn't wish to be a burden on her friends, she approached the school principal about her dilemma. Being a considerate principal he realised that there were many other sole parents within his school community who probably had the same difficulties. As a result he ensured that free child-care was available for parent meetings, social functions and other special events that required parent participation.

It's vital to keep in contact with friends, develop personal interests and stimulate yourself as an adult. Use your support network to give you a regular break so that you can maintain yourself as a person. Children can consume so much of your time and energy that they can leave you feeling physically worn out and mentally drained. Make time to refill the tank so that you can feel revitalised. Do it for your children and for yourself.

Dealing with other people's perceptions

'I must keep up the illusion that I'm coping. It's important to my ego', a single mum recently exclaimed. Sole parents as a group suffer from an image problem. They believe that despite the increase in the number of single parents, they are still not accepted as part of the mainstream and don't properly represent the ideal family model. They are often maligned in the media, and are often indirectly linked to troublesome behaviour of young people.

No model is right or wrong, let alone ideal. We all raise our children in the best way we can under the given circumstances. Other people's opinions or perceptions of us do not or should not affect the way we raise our children. We are the only people who can influence our actions, so it's important to treat ourselves kindly and reduce the pressure that expectations of other's place on us.

A recently separated parent, Christina felt enormous pressure to maintain the impression that she was coping well as a sole parent. As she juggled a full-time professional position with raising four school-aged children, she soon found time in short supply. Among other things she was unable to maintain a neat and tidy house. Christina compromised between the need to keep up a public appearance and practicality. The front lawns were always mown, for the benefit of nosy neighbours, and she ensured that at least the living room was tidy so that she could entertain visitors.

Christina claimed that such action was like putting an advertisement in the newspaper stating, 'I am doing okay as a sole parent'. A sensible solution!

What about my sex life?

Companionship fulfils a basic human need to love and be loved. Children can provide this to a certain extent, but adults generally seek relationships with other adults, which can vary from platonic friendships to close liaisons that satisfy the need for intimacy and sexual contact. The dilemma for many sole parents is to balance their own need for intimate relationships with the wish to provide stability for their children.

Feelings of guilt are common. Parents often believe they should be denying themselves for the sake of their kids. Some sole parents deny this side of their being altogether in an effort to keep their lives uncomplicated. This is a natural reaction when they have been through an emotional wringer during a recent separation. Others put their sex lives on hold for a period of time until their lives, and those of their children, return to a semblance of normality.

Sole fathers generally find it easier than sole mothers to develop sexual relationships. Children, particularly boys, do not see their mothers as sexual beings. A single mother told of the efforts of her teenage son to sabotage her attempts to establish a relationship with another male. When she announced that she was going out for the night, he would pretend to be ill or make up an excuse to keep her at home. He was rude to male guests who entered her home and generally made his mother feel cheap with comments about her behaviour.

This mother felt as if she were a child answerable to a parent. Her son was undoubtedly jealous, as he felt he was being replaced as the family male by an outsider. Regardless of his motives, he was certainly making it difficult for his mother to enjoy a close relationship with a male. This boy had no problems with his father's involvement in a number of sexual relationships with other women.

So you have found a new person in your life? The big question is: When do you tell the children? There is no simple answer; however, it's important that their sense of security is maintained. If you believe that your new relationship is stable, then be open and frank with your children in a manner appropriate to their age and maturity. Help them to understand that the new person in your life will not take you away from them or replace an access parent. Discuss with them how important this person is in your life. Talk to them about the way they might relate to this person, decide on how to refer to him or her (sometimes children do not know what to call a parent's new partner) and how often they may expect to see your partner.

'Why does mum want to bring someone else onto the scene? We were getting along just fine.' Don't be surprised if your children are distant with your new partner until they get to know him or her. As sole parents' relationships with their children are often intense, kids can be hurt or surprised when a new partner enters the scene. It is helpful for your kids to spend time with both of you together, so that they can get to know your companion and see first hand how important you are to each other. Be patient, as it can sometimes take a while to get used to mum or dad not being a single act any more.

What if the children don't get on with my new partner? There is every chance that your kids will not feel the same way as you about your new partner despite his or her efforts to get to know them. If this is the case, encourage youngsters to voice their concerns about your new partner. Listen carefully and understand the reasons for their resentment. They may feel disloyal to a natural parent if they accept your partner, or they may feel that this person will disrupt the relationship that both of you have. It may also be that by disliking your partner a youngster is retaliating against you. Talk through the concerns with your kids and let them know how important this person is to you.

Sometimes initial resentment will not evaporate but that does not excuse rude behaviour. Explain clearly to children how they should behave toward your partner. While you shouldn't expect them to like the new person in your life they should treat them in a civil manner.

Encourage your new partner to take an interest in your children but don't expect this person to be a martyr if the children snub him or her. It may be that the best you will get from either party is politeness. At least it's a start.

Sleep-overs

So your new partner wants to stay the night? Having a new partner sleep the night and wake up in your home is a big step that needs to be taken with care. It can be a shock for younger children, who often see their parents as non-sexual beings. Having a friend stay the night can also indicate that a relationship is becoming serious, which can be the cause of considerable resentment.

Stability and sensitivity are the two keys to dealing with this dilemma. It is important that you as a sole parent provide a stable home life for children and that you are sensitive to their needs and feelings. Many sole parents find it easier to have friends stay the night when children are on access visits. It makes life a lot less complicated for everyone.

If you are going out for the night, arrange it so that your kids can stay with a relative or friend until morning. This allows you to have the luxury of the entire night and morning to do as you wish.

If relatives are in short supply, organise a reciprocal arrangement with a sole parent friend. Swap children for a sleep-over on a regular basis so that you can both benefit from a night and morning to yourselves.

Setting an example

We are role models for children, both now and in the future. The behaviour we display today may well be copied in ten or fifteen years. Just as we generally learn from our own parents so will our children use us as a reference point when they are old enough to have physical relationships.

It's wise for sole parents to use discretion if they are involved in casual sexual relationships, as standards can easily be misinterpreted by your offspring. As one young teenager stated, 'It's okay for mum to sleep around, but yet she won't let me sleep with my boyfriend at home'. Regardless of the accuracy of this assessment, this teenager is using her mother as a model for her own sexual behaviour.

Many sole parents worry that their children will not be exposed to role models of both sexes. This need not be a concern as friends, relatives and grandparents can be worthy substitutes for absent role models. In particular, the parents of your child's closest friends can be readymade role models. Enlist their support and provide opportunities for reciprocal sleep-overs and outings that will enable your kids to have further contact with them.

Teachers can also be excellent role models. Contact your children's school and discuss your concerns with the principal. Placing a child in a class taught by teachers of a particular sex may help to redress an imbalance.

Finding role models for boys

A common concern for many sole mothers is the availability of well-adjusted role models for boys. If their father is not around or they don't have access to male teachers, contact with males can be limited. You may be lucky and have relatives or family friends who are available and willing to spend some time around your sons. Or you may have a family friend who includes your son in his family's activities from time to time. Finding suitable gender role models is a challenge for many mothers particularly as their sons move into adolescence and are looking for men to show them the way. Often relationships can happen in a natural way through shared or common activity. Some boys are drawn toward a respected sports coach or the father of one of their friends.

While it is hard to artificially engineer such relationships, you can make it easier for your sons to find mentors by your willingness to accept such a relationship should one occur and provide opportunities for them to be around other males. It is worth noting that many sons in dual parent families look to male mentors outside their immediate families when they reach adolescence, so finding appropriate male models is not an issue specific to sole mothers.

Relationship with the other partner

The main contact children have with their non-custodial parent is through access visits. These are generally one weekend every fortnight. This provides them with the chance to continue and develop their relationship with that parent. Access visits can be unsettling for parents and children. Kids frequently find that weekend activities such as sports are difficult to maintain.

One boy complained to me that he was unable to play football with a local team on Saturday mornings as he was away with his father every second week. He loved visiting his father but regretted the inconvenience access visits caused.

Help children to prepare for each visit by encouraging them to take toys, books and mementos that they can share with their non-custodial parent. Some children can be unsettled when they return, as the access visit is a reminder of the family life they once knew. Such feelings require patient and careful handling. Give children some time to settle in on their return, and restrain yourself from pumping them for information about the visit. Children will generally tell you in their own time.

Children generally love both parents unconditionally. They don't need to hear one parent being critical of the other. Comments such as 'Your father can be so rude sometimes' or, 'That's typical of her. What do you expect?' are hurtful. They must be able to maintain close relationships with both parents, free from the bitterness that their parents may be experiencing. If there are concerns about the way the other parent is caring for them on access visits, take it up directly with your ex-partner. Don't use the children as a go-between.

'What a terrific report! Why don't you ring dad

tonight and tell him about it? He would be thrilled.'
Encourage kids to maintain contact with their non-
custodial parent on an ongoing basis. When children
have problems or difficulties, or when they have something to share, such as a good report card, if appropriate
you may suggest that they call the other parent. There
are many opportunities for children to keep in contact
with the other parent. It's vital that personal parental bias
or animosity doesn't prevent children from having contact
with their non-custodial parent.

Access visits

**'Twelve days on, two days off' is how one mother
recently described sole parenting.** Access usually
occurs every second weekend and over longer periods of
time during school holidays. Access or non-custodial
parents tend to be males, as fathers are still rarely given
custody of children following a separation.

**Access visits are a lifesaver for most custodial
sole parents.** The weekend away from children belongs
to them. It's their opportunity to do whatever they want —
read and recover, put their feet up, paint the town or
spend intimate time with a companion. They don't have to
be home at a certain time to mind the children, or prepare
meals. Access time is a welcome opportunity for some
well-deserved self-indulgence.

A sole mother described how she spent her children's
first few access visits — worrying about what her ex-
partner may be telling them. She was concerned about

his influence and the untruths he may have told them about her. She soon found that though her suspicions may have had some grounding, her children were happy when they returned home. Besides, she was worrying about something over which she had no control. She learned to relax and use access visits as a weekend off-duty.

Keep access visit arrangements and finances separate. Frequently, access details are confused with financial arrangements. It's the children's right to visit a parent, regardless of whether the parent has met a financial commitment or not. As a rule, try not to discuss finances and access arrangements in the same conversation. This may mean making two phone calls in the same day, but it's worth the effort.

'I don't have to wash the dishes at dad's place.' 'Dad's not mean like you. I want to live with him.' Children's arrival from access visits is often a difficult time for parents. Feelings of resentment and divided loyalty are extremely common. They can be sulky and moody for some time after an access visit. There is little you can do but be understanding and refrain from pushing them for information. Many children can be extremely hurtful to their parents when they compare households or the two parents.

Hurtful statements are common and should not be taken too seriously unless the kids are old enough to decide their own living arrangements. You are more likely to be on the receiving end of such remarks as you are not going to reject them and turn them away. This however doesn't make the remarks any less hurtful.

'Dad took us to the zoo and bought us lunch and an ice-cream. What are we doing next weekend, mum?' Avoid trying to compete with access parents who frequently enjoy great activities with their children. Feeling jealous is natural but unhelpful. Access parents often feel compelled to provide wonderful experiences for their children as they are trying to pack a great deal into one weekend. Be grateful that the children are enjoying themselves at someone else's expense.

What about access parents?

Access parents are in an unenviable position. They see their children in spurts and frequently miss many of the important moments in their kids' lives. They often feel that they have little control or have lost the ability to influence their children. They are unable to leave that special stamp or impression on children's lives that they hoped for at birth. If the access parent has stepchildren, he may feel that he has to prove his love for his children. It's little wonder that many non-custodial parents believe that their children are growing away from them.

It's important to use access visits to really learn about your children and develop your relationship. Ideally, access visits should be a natural slice of life for kids. Aim to integrate your child's life with your own over the two days. Let them do some activities that you normally do so they can learn a little about your life. Give your kids time to settle in when they arrive and resist the temptation to question them about their week the second they arrive. It takes time for them to adjust to a different environment so allow them the time and space to get used to being with you.

When you are all relaxed, conversation will flow more easily. Talk to your children about their interests, their triumphs and disappointments, school and their friends. Listen avidly and give them your full attention. Find a common ground for you to develop a relationship with each of your children.

An acquaintance who has access to his two children each second weekend ensures that he shares an experience with each of his children. He shares a love of sport with his son and he develops this by frequently taking him to sporting events. His daughter is a horse fanatic so he often takes her horse-riding at a nearby equestrian centre. He even learned to ride so he could share this time with his daughter. His children associate their respective interests with their father who, in turn, has an excellent rapport with his offspring.

If possible, provide a space in your home that belongs to your children. This helps them feel that they are not intruders and that they are permanently welcome in both homes. It helps if they have their own bed, cupboard or room so that they have some territorial rights. Children may even have a set of toys or belongings at each home. This helps reduce the feeling that they are living out of a suitcase every second weekend.

Access parents are sometimes reluctant to discipline their children as they feel that if they are too hard on them they may not wish to return. It's important for the children's stability for rules to be established and order to be maintained. Kids will respond accordingly if the rules are fair, their application consistent and your relationship is sound. Many access parents fear significant quarrels or disagreements with their children as they cannot be patched up until the next visit. This is more common in the early years following a separation.

'What is that woman doing?' 'Doesn't your mother buy you any new clothes?' Just as custodial parents worry about the conditions that children live in and the type of influence they are exposed to on access visits, non-custodial parents have similar concerns about their children. Avoid making such comments to your children; instead, discuss your concerns with your ex-partner.

You probably have little control over your ex-partner's methods of parenting, which can be difficult to come to terms with. However, there is little point worrying about something you cannot control. Put your energy into your own parenting for the brief time you are with your kids, and find opportunities to remain in contact during the time you are away. Within reason, encourage your kids to phone or write to you so that you can share many of the aspects of their lives that you are missing.

Chapter 12

THE STEPPARENT'S DILEMMA

'What have I got myself into?' Tom thought to himself. He had just received the cold-shoulder again from sixteen-year-old Dean, his new stepson. Tom reflected on how life was far less complicated before he began a relationship with Kaye two years ago. He has tried to be friendly to her two teenage children but he has always felt that they have resented his intrusion into their lives. Dean, in particular, who has been the sole male in the family for six years, has been difficult to get close to. He rejects any form of discipline that Tom tries to impose.

Tom also reflected on the lukewarm reception that his own nine-year-old son, Damon, receives when he visits every second weekend. He doesn't expect his stepchildren to lay out the red carpet; however, they could at least be civil. He is aware that Kaye is unsure how to react when her children are rude to him, and that she resents feeling that she should take sides with either Tom or her children. Tom reassures himself with the thought, 'It's only early days. Things will work out'.

Stepfamilies are not the same as intact families. A stepfamily is formed when one or both partners have at least one child with another partner with whom they maintain regular contact. Stepchildren can either live with the family full time or visit on a regular basis. One or both partners can bring children into the new family. Stepfamilies are formed in different circumstances and their shapes differ greatly. For instance, children in stepfamilies often have three or four sets of grandparents and such a complex extended family that children have difficulty working out the relationships between people.

In a sense a stepfamily is an instant family. Parents and kids are thrown together with little opportunity for relationships to develop over time as they do in a natural or intact family. Parents have less time together alone to develop their relationship like other new couples. They frequently spend more time developing relationships with children than with each other. It is unrealistic to compare the circumstances of a stepparent with those of a natural parent.

Stepfamilies are formed from loss. Members of stepfamilies have generally experienced some pain or grief as their original family has changed. A sense of loss is common for stepchildren. A new family often leads to further dislocation — usually just as children have adjusted to life with a sole parent. Some resent the formation of a new family, fearing that their old one will disappear while others welcome a stepparent into their lives. **Children experience a variety of emotions when a stepparent enters their lives.** Anger, resentment and guilt are common, particularly if there has been little time or thought given to allow the children to adjust to the idea of a new parent. Kids often feel that they are being disloyal to their natural father if they welcome a stepfather. Others feel a sense of abandonment by a parent who remarries or establishes a new relationship. As their parent is absorbed by their new partner, the children may feel neglected or even cheated. 'Why does mum want to bring him into our house? I thought we were getting along just fine', claimed a resentful eight-year-old battling to come to grips with the idea of sharing his mother with someone else.

'You're not as much fun as my real dad.' Children, resenting the intrusion, often compare a stepparent to their natural parent. 'My dad doesn't make me do that when I visit him.' Such comments hurt, but it must be remembered that kids don't choose their stepparents. They are not consulted and often feel far more loyalty to their natural parents than to a new arrival.

Live-in stepfathers are more common than stepmothers. As most children live with their mothers after a separation, stepfathers generally have less difficulty than stepmothers establishing relationships with stepchildren. Males who establish relationships through play and shared activity are more easily welcomed by young children.

Who needs an outsider? 'We're coping well and don't need you, thanks very much.' However, stepfathers frequently experience difficulty forming relationships with teenagers, males in particular. They can be viewed as unwelcome authority figures by teenage boys, who see their dominant male role being replaced. Stepfathers also find it difficult to establish a place in a well-established, sole-parent family. Roles have been defined, duties assigned and routines in place which enable the family to function smoothly.

Stepmothers frequently have difficulty establishing relationships with stepchildren. Traditionally, mothers adopt the role of nurturer in the family. This is difficult for a stepmother, particularly when this role is already filled. The hardest relationships to be formed are those between stepmother and stepdaughter. The latter often resent a stepmother who tries to behave like a mother, particularly when their own mother is still alive.

Stepmothers often find it difficult when children come for access visits. They are frequently unsure of their role and are required to help children feel welcome while the regular family routine is disrupted. Often stepmothers feel neglected as the father spends a great deal of time with his children, to the detriment of other family duties.

Blended families

Merging two families is usually a complicated affair. Not only is it difficult to define who is actually a member of the family or not, but not everyone wishes to be part of a new family. Some children may grieve for their former family, some may feel unwanted and others may not like the notion of their natural parent being involved in a relationship. The two families probably have different habits, customs and traditions. Everyone in the new family must adjust to the new situation.

A significant change for children in merged or blended families is that the hierarchical structure alters. This can be distressing for children who find that they are displaced from valued family positions. A child who finds that he is no longer the eldest may well resent the older stepsibling, his new family and his natural parent for bringing about the change. Similarly, a child who finds that he is no longer the baby of the family can be perturbed when his cute ways have little effect in the blended family. It's no wonder that conflict and friction are commonplace in newly formed stepfamilies.

It can take years before stepsiblings become integrated into a family. Generally, relationship difficulties between siblings are worked out well before stepparent/stepchildren problems are resolved. This is largely due to the fact that siblings tend to deal with their conflict more openly. They will argue and fight and learn to work out their differences. Often adult/child differences are not tackled in such a way and are left unresolved.

Family meetings are a great way to deal with difficulties. They provide a forum for kids to deal with conflict, establish routines and discuss family rules in a calm atmosphere (see pages 64–6 for how to go about it). Parents have an opportunity to offer suggestions at family meetings but they should refrain from trying to control children. It is essential that they work out their difficulties themselves. Family meetings have the advantage of ensuring that parents do not appear to take sides with their natural children. It is the group that rules, not mum or dad.

Think in terms of 'our' family. A blended family needs to establish its own identity and build its own memories. Regular, enjoyable outings are a terrific way to integrate the family and establish a tradition built on fun and sharing. Such outings do not have to be expensive, but they do need to be planned well in advance as disruptions are commonplace. Encourage children to help plan these outings. It is important that children start to believe that they can contribute to the family's organisation. They need to start thinking in terms of 'our' family.

'He's my dad, not yours.' Kids can resent sharing their parent with other children. It is a good idea to regularly spend some time with your offspring away from stepchildren. Reassure them that they are very special and are not being replaced by stepsiblings. But avoid the temptation of taking sides with your own children when disputes occur. Not only will this be seen as meddling by stepchildren, it is robbing both sides of the opportunity to resolve their own problems.

'Call me mum/dad.' Some stepparents insist on being called mum and dad. This can be extremely distressing to some children who feel that they are being disloyal to their natural parent, even though they may have no contact with that person. Discuss name choices with children so that they feel comfortable with the way they address their stepparents.

Legally, children retain their original surname. Many children resent having surnames changed following a divorce or when they enter a stepfamily. However, if mum takes a new surname children frequently adopt that surname for the sake of convenience. It can be tiring continually explaining to others why you don't carry the same monicker as your mother. Older children often like to keep their original surname as a reminder of their heritage. When deciding on surnames discuss the long-term effects with children and help them to reach a sensible decision. The choice of surnames can be confusing for some children, so patience and understanding is essential.

Merging a natural family with a stepfamily
He's my brother

A common type of stepfamily which receives little recognition is the union between a person with children from a previous relationship and a person with no children. For a time they operate like any stepfamily, with the kids being raised by a step- and a natural parent. Then the couple's own child is born and the dynamics are changed for good. Not only is the birth of a baby a visible bond between parents, but it's also a common link between stepchildren and a stepparent. The arrival of a child should signal a new family unit incorporating all the kids that live in the house — our family.

Some natural parents can become very possessive about the new arrival. They want to do everything for the child and in the process push the stepchildren, and sometimes even the partner, away. This is a natural reaction in some ways but it can be detrimental to family harmony if it continues.

Divided loyalties. In many families there is a large age gap between stepchildren and natural children, or the stepkids only visit once every two weeks. Often the stepkids are old enough to leave home and feel little affiliation or loyalty to you or their stepbrothers or sisters. In some ways you may feel that there are two families existing side-by-side — the step- and the natural children. In these situations your loyalty to your stepchildren may be sorely tested. Feelings of guilt are common as the natural mother feels that she should be doing more for her stepchildren but that they don't want her help, or that they are making life difficult for her and/or the natural child. Some step-parents may even yearn for a 'normal' family life free from the hassles of raising someone else's kids.

A sensible solution. Jackie felt torn between trying to raise her own children and dealing with her stepchildren who visited each fortnight. She tried extremely hard to make her stepsons feel welcome in her home, but they resented her for taking their dad away and made life difficult for her two preschool-aged children. After four years of trying to include her stepkids, Jackie gave up, took her own children out of the house during access visits and gave her husband time and space to be with his sons. The family was never going to be a successful stepfamily so for two days a fortnight both parents spent time alone with their natural children.

Reasonable expectations

Stepparents need to establish realistic goals. 'I expected family life to be great. I wasn't prepared for all the aggravation', exclaimed Tomas.

Tomas went into his marriage with Nadia with blinkers on. It was his first marriage and Nadia had two primary school children from her previous marriage. Nadia's children made Tomas feel like an interloper. As he had no children of his own he was new at parenting. His inexperience added to the insecurity he felt when the children rejected him.

Tomas wanted very much to love and be loved by his stepchildren like a natural father. He didn't take into account that they already had a father they loved very much and whom they visited every second weekend. If he had taken the time to get to know them, he would have learned that they wanted to see more of their natural father and were upset that their mother discouraged phone contact with him.

Tomas was bound to be disappointed by his marriage, as his expectations for his new family and himself were unrealistic. He didn't make allowances for the difference in nature between a stepfamily and an intact family. That's not to say that its members will not be happy and relate well to each other, but to expect too much is courting disaster.

Never try to replace a natural parent. Children will generally reject this, particularly if they have fond memories of the parent you're trying to replace. Children can easily grasp the concept that they have two parents and a stepparent.

All that stepparents can reasonably expect is to be treated with respect and courtesy, especially if the kids are teenagers. Relationships between stepparents and children take time. They will not happen overnight or because they have spent a few pleasant weekends having fun together. Trust and mutual respect cannot be forced or rushed. This can be extremely frustrating for stepparents, such as Tomas, who have unrealistic expectations of life in a stepfamily.

Developing relationships

Couples have to establish two types of relationships. There is the emerging partner relationship and there is the bond developed with children, and these relationships are often at odds with each other. Couples, when they have made the decision to live together, often devote all of their time fostering harmonious adult/child relationships at the expense of the partnership.

The most important relationship is the couple relationship. This partnership is priority number one in any family, but more so in a stepfamily as the pressures and difficulties are often more diverse. Children can easily come between a couple if there isn't a developed secure and supportive relationship.

Couples in a stepfamily do not generally have the luxury of learning about each other without children around. It's wise to extend the courting time with a partner in preference to moving in quickly as it can be extremely difficult getting to know a person when there are two or three children in the house. Time is essential to the development of a relationship, yet many step-parents complain that time is in short supply. One stepfather told me that he and his spouse spent more time alone when they lived apart than they do living together. This is hardly surprising as most couples devote the majority of their time to children when they form a stepfamily.

Couples need to value the time they spend alone. Be aware when children use up that time or invade your privacy. Be firm about bedtimes and establish at least one place in the house where you can retreat for a chat, share a drink or simply spend some quiet time together away from children. It is likely that neither partner has experienced a stepfamily before so it's important that both people support and encourage each other as much as possible. Recognise where there may be difficulties and discuss them at length. It sounds simple, however, many second marriages fail because fundamental issues such as competition for affection or dealing with role changes are unresolved.

Stepfamily relationships are easier to develop when there is a long courtship. Children can gradually get used to the idea of mum or dad having another person in their lives. Some activities and outings can include the children so that they can learn about the new partner in a relaxed setting. Children like to see how a new partner relates to their mother or father and are often relieved to learn that the relationship is less tempestuous than the one they may have witnessed between their natural parents. When courting, take an interest in the kids and take the time to get to know them. Give children the opportunity to learn as much about you as they can before you take on the step-parent role.

Don't be a doormat. Relationships between stepparents and stepchildren vary according to children's age, experiences and the nature of the relationship they have with their natural parent. Certainly many stepparents complain of being treated like an outsider when stepfamilies are newly formed. Older children often have difficulty accepting another parent in their lives and don't mind letting them know it. They may leave them out of conversations, discuss past events or even make references to the parent who doesn't live with them anymore. It's important that a stepparent doesn't act like a doormat when kids treat them in such a way. State your concerns with stepchildren and firmly establish behavioural boundaries you can cope with.

Mutual respect is essential. Treat children with respect and let them know you wish to be treated with courtesy too. Most stepparents find that they need to be extremely patient with some kids who find it difficult to accept that mum or dad has brought a new person into the house. It's not the person they are rejecting, rather they object to the idea of sharing their lives with someone else. Tolerance and understanding are needed to help children get used to the idea of having a stepparent. Most children come around to accepting their step-parents into their lives.

Know your stepchild(ren). Take a personal interest in each of the children and learn about their likes and dislikes, share in any of their hobbies and meet some of their friends. Sometimes playing a game can be a great way to form a relationship as communication occurs within the context of play. Try not to appear too pushy or eager to make children like you.

It often takes time to be accepted so take your cues from the children, keep a sense of proportion and ensure that you have realistic expectations about the relationship you form with your stepchildren. Initiate some enjoyable experiences, such as holidays, visits to the cinema or picnics, so that you can enjoy each others' company in a relaxed atmosphere away from home.

'My original dad was really good at fixing things. I wish he was still here. He could fix my bike.' Step-parents who try to compete with a predecessor are bound to be hurt and disappointed. A stepparent cannot hope to replace a natural parent. Sometimes children will idolise a natural parent, especially if he or she is deceased. It can be extremely difficult for stepparents as they feel that they are always walking in someone else's shadow and failing to measure up. Children often bring up ghosts from the past in a way that can really hurt.

Look at the positives you can offer. Instead of comparing yourself to a natural parent, it is better to value yourself and the contribution you can make to the family. Admit that you cannot fix things like their real father, but that no one tells jokes like you do.

It's important to encourage children to develop a good relationship with natural parents through access visits and regular contact. Research shows that children who have a healthy and secure relationship with their non-custodial parent also have a good relationship with their step-parent. Kids don't substitute one father for another — they can still form significant relationships with two male or female parents.

Some children idolise their absent parent. They forget what they were really like and remember all their positive aspects. Stepchildren who have had little contact with natural parents sometimes reject stepparents and yearn to live with their natural parent. It's important that children are encouraged to make contact with their natural parent so that they form an accurate picture rather than an unrealistic one formed through absence. Youngsters who have been denied access to a natural parent often feel cheated and search out the natural parent during adolescence. Children often strongly resent stepparents who have denied them access to their natural parents.

Dealing with the difficulties

It's not all doom and gloom. In highlighting some of the problems that stepparents may face it is important not to lose sight of the many positive aspects of living in a step-family, such as the opportunity to build a new family. The overwhelming evidence from studies is that stepparents can make a significant and satisfying contribution to their families.

Discipline

The most common difficulty facing stepparents is the issue of discipline. What type of discipline should be used? Who should discipline the children? Should I be responsible for correcting the behaviour of my step-children?

Parents frequently have different approaches to raising children (see Chapter 4). One parent may prefer to talk about misbehaviour with children while the other may prefer to act firmly. Due to past experiences one parent may take a very adverse view of a particular way of dealing with misbehaviour. A mother who experienced some form of physical abuse in her previous relationship may reject any form of physical discipline. In many cases the stepparent has had no experience raising children and needs a great deal of guidance from his partner.

Stepparents often don't know whether they should discipline a stepchild or leave it to the natural parent. Stepparents often have a difficult time dealing with the poor behaviour of teenagers, particularly if the misbehaviour is aimed at them. They often feel frustrated when the natural parent refrains from acting on certain misbehaviour or doesn't consider behaviour to be a problem.

'**You're not my father. I'm not going to listen to you.**' Stepchildren frequently rebel if a stepparent is too strict. They resent his attempts at discipline as interference. On the other hand, natural parents may become frustrated by having to deal with all the misbehaviour while the stepparent is still unsure of his place in the family.

United we stand — parents need to support each other when it comes to discipline. Stepfamilies frequently have two sets of rules, depending on which parent is dealing with a behaviour. Clearly this is unacceptable for the well-being of children, parents and the family as a whole. A discipline plan has to take into account all household members. This planned approach can be discussed by the entire family but it needs to be initiated by the parents. Guidelines need to be discussed about dealing with misbehaviour.

Forming a discipline plan for stepparents

Establish guidelines through discussion to deal with the types of misbehaviour you commonly deal with. Partners can discuss disciplinary responses to behaviours that are acceptable to both. The use of behavioural consequences as outlined in Chapter 5 can form the basis of such a discussion. Determine those behaviours that concern only the kids, those that affect everyone and those specifically aimed at one or other of the parents. Plan responses according to the following guidelines:

1 When children own the behaviour they can learn to be responsible by experiencing the natural consequences of their actions. There is little need for adult interference. For instance, sport uniforms that are not placed in the laundry remain dirty and wet.

2 Behaviours that involve children, such as forgetting to do chores, can be worked out by the children. Parental guidance can be given but advice doesn't have to be accepted.

3 Where behaviour is directed at a parent or requires parental intervention, such as coming home late, follow these useful steps:

a) The natural parent should be responsible for discipline along reasonable lines agreed to by the family. The stepparent should not interfere.
b) The stepparent should be responsible for discipline if the natural parent is not present
c) If a behaviour is directed at a stepparent then he should deal with the behaviour himself. The natural parent needs to support the stepparent in such an instance.

I am so tired

Stepparenting is physically and emotionally draining. The difficulties that stepparents face are especially challenging; however, we often overlook the increased workload involved in raising an instant family whose numbers may have doubled literally overnight. Stepfamilies and intact families share many difficulties, yet they tend to be magnified in stepfamilies. For instance, dealing with difficult teenagers gives most parents nightmares; however stepparents have special problems dealing with teenagers who often resent their attempts to discipline them.

'I receive no thanks for all my hard work.' Stepparents frequently complain that they spend a great deal of time and effort raising their stepchildren yet receive little or no thanks or recognition. A colleague of mine who is also a stepfather explained his feelings of resentment when his eleven-year-old stepson invited his natural father to his primary school graduation ceremony.

'I have driven the boy to sport practice twice a week for the last three years. I read with him every night, help him with his homework, drive his friends home after a visit and give him pocket money when he runs short. I am always there for him. Does he invite me to his special event? No, he invites his father. Where is his father when the hard work has to be put in?'

Such sentiments are understandable but hardly productive. My colleague had a right to feel hurt, yet he knew that his stepson had made the right decision inviting his father to such an important occasion. He agreed that such actions are the inevitable cost of being a stepparent. Incidentally, he did take great pride in his stepson's achievements.

Bill, a stepparent, gives a vivid description of the difficulties he faced trying to cater both to his natural and stepchildren.

'I feel constantly tired bringing up my second wife's children as best as I can. They can be a real handful but we get by. The trouble is I feel too tired to be a good dad to my own children when they come to see me. Sometimes Peter, my eldest child, will come around to tell me about the problems he has at school. He is not too bright and he gets teased by the other kids because he can't read too good. It breaks my heart to hear him sometimes. But what can I do? I can listen but that is about all.

The thing that gets my back up most of all is when Peter and Karen come to stay for the weekend, and my second wife's kids play up something awful. They tease them and gang up to give them hell. When my own children visit now we spend as much time away from the others as we can. Sometimes I take them camping but usually we go on outings. You know what? My stepkids hate me for not taking them along. If I do they'll just make life hell for my two. Hopefully, in time the two lots of children can get along so that we can do some things together. I'd like that.

Bill's story is not unique. Like a servant who tries to serve two masters, Bill found that he is worn out in the process and feels unable to serve either family effectively.

Stepparents need their own space. The attrition rate of stepfamilies is high and is due in no small part to the failure of partners to nurture their own relationships. It is evident that if a stepfamily is to be strong the relationship between partners needs to be nurtured. They need to devote time to themselves away from the pressures of stepchildren, natural children, partners and ex-partners. Take up an interest or a hobby that takes you away from the family situation so that you can relax and unwind. The family will benefit from having a more interesting and refreshed person who is willing to put himself first once or twice a week. This is not indulgence, it's common sense.

Be organised

'Organisation is okay for paid employment, public transport systems and banks but I just want to relax in my home away from such restrictions.' This sentiment is true enough but family living generally involves a great deal of work. Often a high level of organisation is at odds with many people's beliefs about family. I have mentioned often throughout this book the importance of organisation and routine. When responsibilities are shared, routines are established and expectations are known, somehow the workload becomes easier.

Successful stepfamilies are generally extremely well-organised groups. Everyone knows what is expected of him or her and all family members are able to assume responsibility for their own well-being. They plan activities well in advance, as children frequently come and go on weekends, as well as throughout the week. Structure and routine are preferable to chaos in any family.

Stepfamilies are hard work. The challenges facing a stepparent are varied but the rewards of successfully living in a blended or stepfamily are immense. Patience, perseverance and open communication with your partner are the greatest allies to achieving success and happiness as a stepparent. This quote from a friend about raising a stepfamily sums it up well: 'It's such hard work. But I just love 'em all to death. You know, I wouldn't change it for the world.'

Chapter 13

BUILDING A STRONG FAMILY

One constant for parents, regardless of the type of family they belong to, is the wish to promote healthy relationships between themselves and their children. Each and everyone of us wants our family to be strong so that it can nurture us and protect our children. But what is it that enables some families to resist life's difficulties while others fall apart? Two researchers, DeFrain and Stinnett, from the University of Nebraska devised a model of strong families drawing on their research into the qualities that effective, healthy families display. Their Family Strengths Model is based on families of different types, shapes and cultures. This model provides a positive view of how strong families operate and encourages parents to focus on building family strengths rather than focusing on deficiencies.

Following are the six characteristics of strong families, including some ideas about how parents may promote those qualities.

Quality number one: High degree of commitment and caring

Members of strong families make it clear that their relationships with each other are of the utmost importance. 'My family comes first' is common utterance for many people. But the key of course, is to try to make sure that work or other distractions do not interfere with family time.

Commitment within a family is also shown through unconditional love. This means that although there may be times when we don't like our children (or our partner) or what they do, we love them anyway — unwaveringly. I have known many parents whose teenage children have become rebellious, abusive or engage in risk-taking activities and they can do little more than be patient and love them. It is astonishing how kids (or young adults) will generally return to their parents or come to their senses because they are aware that their parents love them. One commonality in kids or adults who are able to cope with life's adversities is the existence of at least one person in their lives who has faith in them and has invested emotional energy in them.

Shared experiences also foster commitment within a family. When kids and parents enjoy each other's company, a deeper level of trust is established and a better relationship is fostered. Even simple rituals such as sharing a meal or reading a story increase the level of commitment within a family.

When family members are committed, they don't stifle each other but create sufficient space and encouragement for each to pursue their own goals and interests. Support of others' interests and goals tends to be reciprocal in healthy families and can, in turn, also encourage better communication and enthusiasm for family activities.

Quality number two: Appreciation and affection

People in strong families let each other know through their words and actions that they love and appreciate one another. Physical affection such as hugs and cuddling, and verbal affection tend to be expressed regularly and openly in strong families.

In some cultures it is uncommon to express appreciation and affection openly. Instead these feelings might be expressed indirectly. But the key is that individuals are aware of the positive emotions that others in the family feel for them.

People in strong families do criticise each other but the number of positive strokes far outweighs the negatives. One family, for example, has developed an excellent strategy for keeping their home a positive place. If anyone is critical of another member they match the criticism with five positive comments.

Positive, affectionate exchanges in a family tend to

snowball. If you show your appreciation for the actions of a child or give your partner a hug then the chances of you or another family member receiving similar treatment increase dramatically.

If you are not naturally affectionate or supportive, try linking these behaviours to existing behaviours. For instance, show affection when you say good night to each child and say something positive or appreciative about his or her behaviour.

One way to show affection with adolescents is through touch. Give them a back rub or a shoulder rub on a regular basis. Not only will this draw you closer together but it is a fantastic stress management tool as well. And yes, adolescent boys generally love having their backs rubbed by either mum or dad.

If you are in a couple-relationship be affectionate to your partner. Not only does this provide a good model for your children but there is significant research to suggest that a couple's warm sexual feelings for each other stem from feelings of emotional closeness developed through-out the day.

Quality number three: Positive communication

It seems that the best communication in families occurs when no one is working at it. It occurs as a result of natural interaction rather than forced methods. It is also apparent that a high level of trust is an essential element for effective family communication. When trust is high parents and kids can talk freely about important issues such as sex, drugs or the future.

In strong families communication doesn't always produce agreement. However, family members are able to speak freely and openly with each other without blaming, condemning or being condescending. They will agree to disagree or work at a compromise but they will not become hostile or hold grudges. Members of strong families get on with life and recognise that they are responsible for their own actions and opinions.

Members of strong families are generally very good listeners. They are likely to listen to other people's points of view and ask questions rather than try to read other people's minds.

Humour is an important part of functioning families, too. The stronger the family, the more likely they are to use humour to reduce tension, maintain a positive outlook on life, to express warmth, to facilitate conversation and to help each other cope with difficult situations. Strong families don't use humour negatively so they steer clear of sarcasm and personal putdowns.

Another feature of positive communication in strong families is the ability to give compliments and positive feedback for activities, behaviour or good performance. Kids' efforts are recognised, and encouragement rather than bribery is given to induce good behaviour or better schoolwork.

Strong families also focus on finding solutions rather

than laying blame when things go wrong. If a child makes a mess, positive communication focuses on cleaning it up rather than chastising the culprit. If he gets in trouble with the law, parents will look at how the child can change rather than focus on reprimanding him or her. While obviously accountability for behaviour is important, strong families look forward rather than back.

Members of strong families feel that it is permissible to share negative as well as positive feelings. They find acceptable ways of voicing their feelings and are more likely to use assertion than aggression when they are angry. It is important to develop the notion that there are no feelings that are unacceptable in a family, but there are unacceptable behaviours.

Quality number four: Attendance given to spiritual wellbeing

Of the six qualities of healthy families spiritual wellbeing is the most difficult to pinpoint because spirituality means different things to different people. Cross cultural research shows, however, that although families attribute their spiritual wellbeing to different origins and use different language to express spirituality it is apparent that a connection with something deeper than flesh and blood increases a family's resilience.

Some families talk about faith in God, while others see God in nature or the eyes of their children. Some describe feelings of hope, peace and optimism in their lives. Some say they feel a oneness with the world, while others talk in religious terms, describing the love they feel for each other as sacred. Many express these kinds of feelings in terms of universal values such as fairness and generosity.

The elusive concept called spiritual wellbeing is about connection. Connection to each other and connection to that which is sacred in life. Families strengthen their spiritual wellbeing in their own ways: those connected through formal religions do this through the various rituals that they participate in and that become a part of their family life; those parents who don't have strong links to formal religion strengthen spiritual wellbeing, (as do families with strong ties to formal religion) when they promote sharing, love and compassion — making these values come alive in their daily lives.

The notion of spirituality is not found in many parenting manuals, where the focus tends to be on behaviour management, self-esteem, communication and relationship building. The issue of promoting kids' spiritual wellbeing is rarely mentioned, but obviously is no less important. And with exposure to marketing and advertising reducing most things in kids' lives to commercial value, the idea of spirituality is harder than ever to promote in today's more street-wise kids.

But there are places outside the family where children can attain a wider sense of spirituality. My children's secondary school, for example, constantly promotes three values: Respect yourself, Respect others and Respect the environment. This Holy Trinity of

Respect is the foundation of all rules and all relationships that occur within the school. These values promote a sense of spiritual wellbeing as they remind kids not only of their responsibility to look after themselves and others but also of their connection to something bigger than themselves.

Quality number five: Time together is valued

An important reason a family remains strong and connected is because they do things together that are enjoyable for everyone. At present Australian families are time-strapped, as they are in most Western countries. It is increasingly difficult for families to participate in basic activities such as eating a meal together or just 'hanging out' as a family.

Many families appear to settle for quality time at the expense of quantity time. But the notion that parents should spend small amounts of high quality time with their children just doesn't make sense. Intimacy doesn't occur in small parcels. You have to be around kids for a while to really connect and build up a high emotional bank account.

The critical issue, however, is not so much the time you spend in the company of your kids (though it is important) but exactly what you do with your kids when you are with them and how you do it. Do you engage in activities that are enjoyable for them, that involve play and laughter, or are all your interactions with children serious and of a managerial nature? But even mundane managerial activities can be made enjoyable. Last week, for example, I spent time cleaning the house with my two daughters and we ended up having a huge pillow fight. Okay, I started it but I couldn't resist it! It is often through everyday interactions with children that connections are made, so it's important to embrace these opportunities for family fun when they arise.

Research by John DeFrain has found that the happiest childhood memories that adults hold have two common threads. First, childhood happiness almost always centres on activities experienced together as a family. Second, the most pleasurable childhood times almost always centre on simple, inexpensive activities. Money can't buy happiness, but loving family relationships can create it.

Quality number six:
The ability to cope with stress and crises

Strong families are not immune to experiencing difficulties but they possess the ability to cope with crises.

Another study conducted by John DeFrain focused on how 81 strong families coped with crises. Twenty-three per cent suffered a serious illness in the family, 21 per cent claimed a death in the family and, coming in third, were marital problems. These were the three most difficult issues that this group of families had to face.

Amazingly, 96 per cent of the families said they were successful in meeting these challenges. The most common strategy used was to pull together and develop a strong sense of teamwork rather than pull apart. The family crises and stresses in effect strengthened the bonds that already existed.

Also, members of these families sought out help when they were in difficulty. They attended counseling sessions or used their broader social networks for assistance. There is a clear suggestion that families which are unable to admit they are having difficulty, and so don't seek advice, are more at risk of breaking down.

Strong families are generally resilient, more adaptable to change and can grow even in the hardest of economic or social environments. And the keys to resilience lie in the development of the other five qualities of strong families: commitment to each other; open, positive communication; showing appreciation and affection for each other; spending enjoyable time together; and attention to spiritual wellbeing. Families which focus on developing these strengths are more able to respond to crises and stress in ways which sustain and strengthen.

A final word

It is by building family strengths rather than focussing on weaknesses that parents can really impact on their families in long-term beneficial ways. Often our parenting concerns are day-to-day managerial issues, dealing with kids when they are less than perfect or such mundane issues as getting them off to school on time. It is true that this is the stuff of childrearing. But while we are involved with children at this basic level we must also recognise our opportunities for building a strong family and take them. As families are the building blocks for community and form the essential support mechanism for individuals, when families are strong then communities and societies will be strong. And so too will our children be strong.

The Michael Grose Parenting Series
from Random House

A Man's Guide to Raising Kids
At last a parenting guide specifically written for men in the 21st century. Michael Grose provides positive and practical advice on how to manage your busy schedule and still be a great dad. This book shows how to make the most of the special place you hold in your children's lives, and make it fun!

One Step Ahead: Raising 3–12 Year Olds
Good parenting isn't instinctive. It's often done by trial and error. But a little guidance as to what you can expect from young children goes a long way towards helping you confidently deal with the problems that arise. Michael Grose identifies the many and varied problems parents most often encounter, including bed-wetting, fussy eaters, sibling rivalry, swearing and tantrums, and helps you stay one step ahead.

Working Parents
Many working parents think there's no such thing as a balanced life. But Michael Grose—having learnt the hard way—can show you there is. This book debunks those 'perfect working parents' myths, and instead provides commonsense advice and easy tips on how to maintain quality time, beat guilt, and keep on top of the chaos, showing that you can not just survive but thrive as busy mums and dads.

Why First Borns Rule the World and Last Borns Want to Change It
Why is it that children in a family can share the same gene pool, a similar socio-economic environment and experience similar parenting styles yet have fundamentally different personalities, interests and even different careers as adults? Birth order! This book provides answers to all your questions about the personality and behaviour of your colleagues, life partner, friends, siblings and children. And, perhaps explains some of your own ambitions and quirks.